m

J

RED MOON PASSAGE

RED MOON PASSAGE

The Power and
Wisdom
of Menopause

BONNIE J. HORRIGAN

Harmony Books / New York

Published by Harmony Books, a division of Crown Publishers, Inc., 201 East 50th Street, New York, New York 10022. Member of the Crown Publishing Group.

Random House, Inc. New York, Toronto, London, Sydney, Auckland
http://www.randomhouse.com/

HARMONY and colophon are trademarks of Crown Publishers, Inc.

PRINTED IN THE UNITED STATES OF AMERICA

Design by Cathryn S. Aison

Library of Congress Cataloging-in-Publication Data
Horrigan, Bonnie J.
Red moon passage : the power and wisdom of menopause / by
Bonnie J. Horrigan. — 1st ed.
Includes bibliographical references and index.
1. Menopause—Psychological aspects. 2. Menopause—Social
aspects. I. Title.
RG186.H675 1996
618.1'75'0019—dc20   96–4122

ISBN 0-517-70386-6

10 9 8 7 6 5 4 3 2 1

FIRST EDITION

This book is for those of us who share the feminine spirit,
who were born from its graces, its passions,
and its challenges.
And it is especially for those brave women
who will sing the new feminine dreaming into being.

This book is also dedicated to my mother,
Mrs. Angela Aiello Duvall,
who taught me the miracle of unconditional love.

·❨ ACKNOWLEDGMENTS ❩·

As I LOOK BACK on the past, on the path that finds me here, I see how my life is inescapably intertwined with the lives of others. I stand alone but am also part of everyone I know, just as they, standing alone, are part of me. So while I take credit for the creation of this book, I also must give credit.

I would like to thank my husband, David John Horrigan, for his selfless love for me, for his support and great wisdom. David's gift is the magic of love and compassion, the magic of transformation. I would like to thank my son, Jean-Paul Alexander Horrigan, who chose to be part of my life and thus part of the story of this book, and in so doing brought great joy into my world. I would like to thank my father, Wilbur I. Duvall, who taught me the value of integrity and showed me that the human mind can be used to solve problems.

I would also like to thank my agent, Stephanie Tade, for her belief in this book and support of me as an author and the wonderful people at Harmony Books, particularly Leslie Meredith, Sherri Rifkin, and Karin Wood, for bringing *Red Moon Passage* into being.

Thanks must also be given to the eight women who joined me in this endeavor: Jeanne Achterberg, Paula Gunn Allen, Angeles Arrien, Clarissa Pinkola Estés, Kachinas Kutenai, Carol Pearson, Jamie Sams, and Barbara Walker, and to the authors of the books mentioned in the bibliography.

I also need to thank Larry Dossey for changing my life. One day I asked, "Larry, have you ever experienced a time when your thoughts actually affected the world?" And he so wisely answered, "Bonnie, I don't think I have experienced a time when they haven't."

·⟨ CONTENTS ⟩·

·《 INTRODUCTION 》·

THIS BOOK IS ABOUT the transitional time most American women call menopause but which I have renamed the Red Moon Passage. Menopause is a negative term. It is derived from the Greek word *meis* meaning "moon" and the French word *pause* meaning "pause." Menopause means the cessation of menstruation and by extension, the cessation of the ability to give birth to new life. Period. End of thought. There is no second, third, or clarifying definition. Consequently, the word focuses a person's attention on a stopping, an ending, and silently infers that nothing exists beyond that end.

But we, my friends, have been led astray. There is something beyond that end. And it is something magnificent.

Red Moon Passage is a phrase I devised. It does not come from any one particular culture. In renaming menopause for myself, I tried to find words that would describe both our growing out of the blood cycles and childbearing years, our indelible physical connection to the feminine, and the fact that as menopause is completed, we enter into a new realm of being. In every way, we are on a voyage to a new land.

The text is based on interviews I conducted with eight extraordinary women who work in the realm of psyche and soul. While these women were born into different cultures and have experienced different ethnic, economic, and social backgrounds, and while the paths they chose to walk are divergent, they share a significant common trait. Years ago, these women dared to question the status quo. They dared to listen to their own intuition and look beyond the superficial facade of life into the innermost core from which all things come. But most important, having looked, they resolved to follow their hearts and build a life based on what they perceived as truth.

To me, each of these women is a hero in her own right. As with Joseph Campbell's quintessential archetype,[1] each embarked on a journey into the dark unknown. After surviving the many challenges, the opposition, the disappointments, the fear, the loneliness, and the pain, each of these women found gifts of wisdom and truth. Having done so, each then returned to the mundane world to teach the knowledge she had learned.

The female tradition, the collective consciousness of womanhood, prospers for their work.

How I met them and why I met them is part of the magical unfolding of my own life and also part of the greater story contained in these pages. In a broader sense, this book is about change and transformation of all kinds, but more specifically, more exactly, it is about menopause and creation.

You may think the pairing of the two ideas to be odd. I did at first. But I invite you to read on and then judge for yourself.

The story begins thousands of years ago in the spring of 1989. That was the cold, wet year I turned forty, and just like my mother and her mother before, as I glided past that particular milestone, my hair started to gray. The silver streak began with just a few renegade strands, but by the time I celebrated birthday forty-one, it was a noticeable fact to anyone who cared to look in my direction with

[1] Campbell, Joseph. *The Power of Myth,* Anchor Books Doubleday, New York, 1988, page 49. "The courage to face the trials and to bring a whole new body of possibilities into the field of interpreted experience for other people to experience—that is the hero's deed."

their eyes focused. This evidence of my age and ultimate mortality saddened me. I felt like I was losing something, and for a short while felt cheated, as if something had not just been lost but had been stolen instead. Then I felt a razor sharp, bone-chilling fear. I was not ready for my glorious youth to be over. I did not want to grow old. I did not want my life to end.

I subjected myself to the torture of self-pity for several months before years of philosophical study and spiritual practice came to my rescue. My deep knowingness rose to the surface and strangled the would-be victim I was well on my way to becoming. The next day, after studying my face in the mirror for three hours, trying to see past my eyes into my soul, I finally reconciled myself to the fact that I was, however regretfully or unregretfully, growing older. But more to the point, I came to grips with the fact that it was something that happened to everyone and everything. People, animals, plants, the earth, the sun—indeed, the entire galaxy was aging. It was a natural phenomenon, part of the life cycle, part of the Divine plan. Armed with this truth, I decided that if I had to have gray hair, then I was going to have *long* gray hair and I would welcome its entrance into my universe as if it were an old and cherished friend.

When I mentioned this idea to my peers, men and women alike, most thought I was crazy. Why suffer the effects of old age, they asked, when modern science could prevent, or at least cover up, the visible truths? Why lose one's girlish figure to middle-age spread when liposuction and plastic surgery were options? Why be gray-headed when the beauty parlor was just down the street? And then, of course, the big question, the most unspoken-about dread: Why endure the emotional and physical effects of menopause when you could take estrogen (and perhaps other drugs) for the rest of your life?

I didn't have immediate answers—at least none that made any sense in the face of their well-documented, well-financed arguments. But what I did have was a feeling deep inside me that all this scrambling to hang on to youth was somehow misguided. It isn't that hair dye or tummy tucks are in themselves inherently bad, because they aren't. I was simply haunted by a sense that *denial* of the aging process prevented the birth of something important.

But what?

The days passed. As my friends laughed their way home from the beauty parlor, my uneasy feelings grew. I kept thinking of the story of the mythic king who drinks the elixir of immortality and dies. Yet the answer to my yearnings seemed to live just outside my grasp.

Then, one evening that summer while sitting alone on my back patio listening to the Colorado night, I experienced a fleeting vision of an old woman. She appeared before me quite clearly as if she were actually standing on the cobblestones and breathing the cool night air. I didn't recognize her as being anyone I knew, but I immediately liked her with an affection that rose from deep inside my bones. She was on in years, perhaps eighty or even ninety. Her hair was completely white, her skin wrinkled, her posture slightly stooped. But her smile was radiant and her eyes were aglow with an unwavering serenity. This woman wasn't in mourning over a bygone youth or living in fear of her impending death. Instead, she was completely at ease with, and quite happy about, who and what she was. But even more, I sensed she was magical. One look into the vast depths of her eyes told me that she knew many things about the world we live in and of the other, invisible world from which our breath comes.

I reached out to her, wanting to ask a thousand questions, but her image flickered and vanished. She was gone as quickly as she came, and I was left alone with only her memory. I sat in the darkness for a long while after, pondering what I had experienced and what had been imparted in those brief few seconds. One thing was certain. The old woman I had seen—white-haired, hobbling, wrinkled as she was—possessed an immense power.

And so the search began.

(PART ONE)

Menopause
as a Journey of Initiation

INSPIRED BY MY VISION OF THE OLD WOMAN, I spent the next week worrying about where and how and when I could find trace of her. She was from the timeless, ethereal, nonlinear world of the soul and I lived in twentieth-century, prove-it-to-me-scientifically America. She came from the realm of miracles. I existed in a culture of rules.

Who would know of her? I wondered. Who would understand the passage I was seeking and comprehend the power that becomes available when the transformation is complete? To whom could I go for help?

Several women came to mind. But in telling this tale, I need to go back in time to my age of innocence—and wisdom—in the early 1950s.

When I was very young, I believed in miracles. I believed in the possibility of wishes coming true and in the ultimate benevolence of the universe. I trusted that the nonordinary could happen, that the future brimmed with impossible possibility, and that what I saw with my imagination was equally real to what I saw with my eyes. During those early years, the world was a magical place and I believed that no matter how small, I played a part in its creation.

Then I grew up.

The celestial light dimmed. The apparent world grew more real and rules more imposing, more difficult to change. I completely forgot that life, in its expansive glory, operated on many levels. Sadly, quietly, I joined the ranks of trained and socialized human beings to whom spirit was dead.

But one strange day during my senior year of high school, while walking down the hall to my English class, for a reason I will never quite know, I woke up. I know of no other way to describe what for me was a startling experience. It was like coming out of a trance or awakening from a dream. There I was in the hallway, suddenly conscious again, aware of life in a deeper way. At that point, a small ray of light broke through the cloud cover. A skeleton rose from the grave.

What followed were years upon years during which I sought out and studied many of the world's major spiritual movements. Very simply, after that experience, I was no longer interested in religious or societal propaganda. I wanted to know how I could stay "awake." I wanted to know the truth about life.

Although I never had the honor to meet most of the following teachers face to face, I did read their books, their essays, their collected work. In this manner, Alan Watts introduced me to Zen Buddhism, Maharishi Mahesh Yogi to Transcendental Meditation, Carlos Casteneda to Indian sorcery, Carl Jung to the collective unconscious, Michael Harner to core shamanism, Joseph Campbell to the realms of myth, George Ivanovitch Gurdjieff to European mysticism, Paramahansa Yogananda to the Self-Realization Fellowship, and Laotse to the way of the Tao.

As I studied these various bodies of knowledge, I began to see an underlying pattern. The words and trappings changed, the cultures of origin changed, but certain fundamental truths were present in all. I soon knew that I wasn't crazy and that I wasn't alone. Spirit was absolutely, positively real.

Still, something was missing. I had a deep yearning for I knew not what. There seemed to be an unnamed potential imprisoned inside me that cried to be released. The years passed. Then I happened upon another great teacher, a woman named Dr. Carol Pearson. Actually I didn't find Dr. Pearson, I found her book—*The Hero Within*. And even more truthfully, I didn't find her book. It found me. It was 1986 and someone thrust it into my hands. I don't remember who now. They simply said, "Here, you have to read this."

The book was so absorbing that I kept turning pages far into the night. Dr. Pearson talked about six archetypes she found common to modern humanity and how we could use these archetypes to understand ourselves and our experiences, and to grow. She explained that these archetypes—Innocent, Orphan, Martyr, Wanderer, Warrior, and Magician—represented patterns of behavior.[1] They are fundamental modes we use to deal with our inner and outer worlds. (An innocent hopes, a martyr makes sacrifices, a warrior goes to battle.) But most important, she said that by knowing which archetypes are active in our lives and by moving this knowledge from the unconscious to the conscious, our personal world can be transformed. We can move from the shadows of reaction into the light of choice.

More than most, this book spoke to me. I began to see the deeper patterns of my behavior, the filters of my mind, and how these filters/behaviors affected my life. As I read on, I found myself exclaiming, "Oh, so that's what's been going on!" But then, in her chapter on the Magician archetype, Dr. Pearson eloquently explained all about the magical world I had lived in as a child.

"The archetype of the Magician," she wrote, "teaches us about creation, about our capacity to bring into being what was never there before, and about claiming our role as co-creators of the universe."[2] She explained how miracles happen through trust in the universe and self, how synchronicity arises from honest connec-

---

[1] *Webster's II New Riverside University Dictionary* defines archetype as a prototype—an original type, form, or instance that is a model on which later stages are based or judged. Also, an early typical example, or a primitive or ancestral form or species.

[2] Pearson, Carol S. *The Hero Within*. Harper & Row, New York, 1986, page 116.

tion, and how we can call our shadows into being to integrate them and thereby change the course of our lives.

I remember lying in bed, barely breathing, heart beating double-time, thinking, "She knows. This lady *knows.*"

Indeed, Dr. Pearson does know. When I started searching for the wise old woman of my vision, I remembered her book. I took it off my bookshelf and reread it for the tenth time. Soon enough I realized that the crone I had seen, whose presence had radiated such life, was Dr. Pearson's Magician. Like the archetype, the old woman was capable of *conscious* co-creation.

It was clear that Dr. Pearson would be able to help me find the old woman, or perhaps it's more exact to say that I knew Dr. Pearson could help me—and anyone else who so chose—to *become* her.

So I wrote Dr. Pearson a letter. She agreed to meet and in the fall of 1992, she talked to me at length about how we can deal with our shadows and make the passage through menopause a positive, transformative experience. She explained that when we take the journey menopause offers and *complete* the crossing, new growth in our souls and our lives will occur.

Hers is the voice of experience speaking. Dr. Pearson has taken many journeys of her own and not unsurprisingly, her personal universe and the world that surrounds her are a bit more alive than one might encounter with others.

I offer this story in explanation.

In November 1992, I had flown to Washington, D.C., and was staying in a downtown hotel. After catching a cab outside the hotel lobby, I handed the driver Dr. Pearson's address. He read the note, nodded, and sped off. Forty-five minutes later he pulled off the Baltimore/Washington Beltway and nervously confessed that we were lost. Incredulous, I dug out a map and discovered that we had in fact missed our turn and gone some twenty-five miles out of our way. When I realized that I was going to be late to one of the most important meetings of my entire life, I began to fume.

The cabbie promptly pretended he didn't speak English.

As I sat in the backseat of the cab, trying not to cry, I suddenly remembered who it was I was going to see. In a synchronistic world, no one is isolated. Events, people, places, things—everything is connected. Trust the process, a voice whispered inside my head. Trust your connection. So I let my anger and frustration go, consulted the map, and then guided the cab driver to College Park. When I finally arrived at her office, Dr. Pearson was, as I suspected she might be, still busy with a client.

So that was how our meeting began, with that synchronistic experience in which her world affected how my world affected hers. Dr. Pearson came out to the reception area shortly thereafter. We made our introductions, talked our small talk, and then moved to her office. As we settled into our chairs, I felt slightly disturbed. We were sitting in *ordinary* chairs. My feet were planted on an *ordinary* rug. Hers was an ordinary office in an ordinary building in a quite ordinary part of town. Yet Dr. Carol Pearson is anything but ordinary. I'm not sure what I was expecting. A golden crown on her head? A ruby-studded robe? I felt like I was in a Zen parable. Here was a great teacher dressed in student clothing.

The conversation that followed was spellbinding. As we discussed menopause and traveled through various worlds of philosophical thought, I felt the boundaries confining my concept of possibility stretch. New paths opened. Previously unseen vistas came into view.

Dr. Pearson's work with human psyche is based on two fundamental principles—the hero's journey as path for transformation and the healing presence of archetypal guides—and it is the combination of these two ideas that I and so many other women have found particularly powerful.

The next part of this text is a transcript of our magical conversation.

And so the teacher speaks.

☘ *Carol S. Pearson* ☘

THE NEW HERO'S JOURNEY

My basic premise on the hero's journey is that we have passed the time in history where there are heroes and everyone else, and the heroes save the day and the rest of us get saved. Instead, we are now in the time when we are *all* heroes and we are *all* on a journey.

Traditionally in the hero's journey, the hero rides out, faces the dragon, finds the treasure, and then returns to transform the kingdom. In the modern world, we each face what we fear and find out who we are. When we have the courage to actually be who we are, then we transform our personal kingdom, and the ripple effect helps to transform the larger kingdom.

In order to make a difference in the world, you need to do your own work. You need to take your own journey and face your own dragons and find your own treasures. And the treasure for the hero's journey is finding out who you are so you can know what your truth is, what your vocation is, and what it is you have to give. If people fail to do that, if they get into performance or trying to measure up or do what advertising says or what the management literature says or what some therapist says or what the church says, then what happens is they end up being a good copy of somebody else and there is an empty space where their own unique gifts could be.

This has all kinds of implications for philosophy and politics because it means that we need *everybody*. It means I can't do your piece and you can't do mine. So it isn't a matter of who's better or who are the important and unimportant ones. It's a matter of finding a way to foster everybody's development.

The call for authenticity in the passage presented by menopause is to find out what is true and real about yourself as a menopausal woman. But before we enter into that discussion, I want to tell you briefly about the other cornerstone of my work—the archetypes.

PRIMAL PATTERNS AS TEACHERS

There are many archetypes, but the ones I work with are the archetypes that help us with the individuation process, with the process of becoming whole and uniquely ourselves.

For instance, if the Wanderer is active in a woman's life, her initial response to a problem might be to leave and embark upon a quest. If the Warrior is active, her probable response will be to stay and fight the problem head-on. A woman living out the Martyr, on the other hand, might sacrifice herself as part of the solution.

The journey is to discover these impulses in ourselves and move them from unconscious to conscious so that we are no longer controlled by them.

What I do is put the Gestalt emphasis on process together with the archetypes of Jungian psychology to say that you can *trust the process of the emergence of the archetypes in your life.* Each archetype has a gift to give you, and when you need an archetype in terms of your development, it will emerge.

If you don't fight it, that is.

However, we typically struggle against experiencing certain aspects of our lives, particularly when what is happening goes against ingrained cultural ideals. We resist things like aging and menopause. We deny their existence and do whatever we can to stop the experience because we have the idea that the experience is bad. Rather than fostering growth, this kind of behavior can result in fear, anxiety, and depression.

MENOPAUSE AS A CONSCIOUS JOURNEY

Currently in our culture, the menopausal journey is charted in a most unsatisfactory way. We lack for positive images, so who wouldn't be scared? But if women see menopause as strictly a physical event, then what they will experience is a narrow band of physical reality involving losing their youth and their ability to give birth. But that is only one dimension of a multidimensional experience. By being conscious of the other, deeper aspects of life, menopause can be experienced as a spiritual passage, and a whole new level of reality can be accessed.

We haven't been given terms to think of menopause as a spiritual passage. And clearly that's what you are on to. But it's not only about being conscious. This passage isn't yet named. And even with this wonderful book it won't be named diversely enough because we are just beginning to remember or invent terms adequate to describing women's experiences.

THE SKILL OF NAMING

The skill of naming is the Magician's skill of defining what an experience is.[3] By naming something correctly, by finding the positive growth aspects despite any pathology, a Magician can transform an experience from bad to good. Magicians can turn limiting circumstances into opportunities and misfortunes into blessings. Like in the tale of *Jerome the Frog*[4]:

> A playful witch tells Jerome she has turned him into a
> prince. He still looks like a frog, but townspeople begin

---

[3]The process of naming is discussed in detail in *The Hero Within* and *Awakening the Hero Within*.

[4]Ressner, Phillip. *Jerome the Frog, Parents* magazine, New York, 1967.

sending him on quests just in case he really is a prince. He has several successes, so they finally send him to slay the dragon, who is always breathing fire and destroying villages. Jerome finds the dragon and draws his sword, but the dragon asks why. It is, after all, his nature to breathe fire and burn villages. Jerome ponders this and they discuss things awhile and finally come up with a solution agreeable to all. The dragon will burn the town garbage every Tuesday and Thursday, and lie around and tell lies the rest of the week. Jerome does not try to convert the dragon or convince him to be "good," but instead helps him to be more fruitfully who he is, since dragons not only love to breathe and burn things up but also like to be admired and appreciated.[5]

Jerome was a Magician. He "noticed" what the dragon was. He "named" the dragon correctly and after he did, the dragon turned from foe to friend. Accordingly, how we "name" menopause for ourselves—terrible? enlightening? frightening? joyous?—will determine how we experience it.

Women need to develop the kind of consciousness of noticing what menopause is. Noticing not only what we are giving up but also what we are moving toward. I think we have done a lot more noticing about what menopause isn't (youth, babies) and about the negative aspects of menopause (wrinkles, gray hair, less energy, decreased bone mass) than we have about menopause's positive elements. And there are positive aspects.

What intrigues me is where menopause leads to. When I look at myself and my colleagues, I see menopause as a call toward autonomy, toward being self-defined as opposed to reactive. For instance, lately I feel less inclined to do things just because other people want me to do them, and I no longer feel like I have to prove myself to anyone or to the world. This translates into having a consciousness in which it is easier to be true to myself.

I also see a desire to simplify, to do less just because it would be nice, and to focus more on what really matters. I think some of that has to do with having less energy. You have to make harder choices. But it also comes from life experience, from having tried enough things to know that not everything that looks good is all that satisfying.

On the other hand, while menopause feels like a journey into autonomy, I've noticed that relationships with my children, husband, and friends have become more important. I'm also experiencing an impatience with dependency. For me, this is new. I simply don't want to be close with people who expect me to take care of them or rescue them. So it's a turn away from a more motherly stance in the world. I'm not talking about codependence. I'm talking about archetypically completing my work in the Caregiver (the loving parent, the nurturer, the earth mother, the tree of life) and moving into some other archetype, at least for the time being.

But while menopause, by its very nature, is a movement away from the Caregiver, it is not a movement out of Lover. The Lover archetype is very much a menopausal experience.

CONTACTING THE FEMININE CONSCIOUSNESS

A colleague of mine, David Oldfield, and I were talking about developing rituals for midlife. He was reading about ancient African rituals where the tribal women had a tradition of letting their breasts hang to announce that they were no longer sexual. But that's not what menopause is for today's women. I've observed women actually finding their sexuality in a new way. They are claiming it as not being about reproduction, not being about making somebody else happy or calling somebody to them, but as a kind of joy for its own sake.

Earlier in life, I was afraid of the feminine because I did not want to be confined by traditional female roles. After having developed a thriving career, I no longer have this fear. Now, in midlife, I'm reclaiming the feminine, but in a way that has nothing to do with the stereotypical definitions of femininity. It is more about a quality of being—of spirit embodied in loving connection with other people, society, the earth.

In Judith Duerk's book, *Circle of Stones,* she writes about longing for an authentic feminine experience of being in the flow of life. What Duerk is talking about is not being rushed, not being in that Yang-pushed achievement mode all the time, and being able to slow down and experience the wonder of life.

I think this has something to do with the true feminine. They say menopause can take ten years. Well, the feminine is about being able to *be* with that process. It's about being with the world, being with your work, being with your significant others and with your own process in a more patient, conscious way.

THE MENOPAUSAL ARCHETYPES

Menopause is a soul journey, and as such it involves the archetypes of Seeker, Destroyer, Lover, and Creator.

When the Seeker archetype is active in your life, you feel your aloneness. You can even feel alienated, but you have a desire to go and seek. You might have the urge to travel or explore new lifestyles or new ideas or to write books and find out about things you didn't know about. You might connect with people who have new and different ideas. Typically, you feel a little confined by the status quo, by the demands to conform, by the culturally dominant paradigms, and the limitations of consensual reality.

Seeker is what propels many of us to think about things differently. It's the call to spirit. It's the archetype that moves us up to connect with something inspirational, something more beautiful and more enriching than our lives.

The Destroyer archetype is the death archetype. Destroyer is the call to go down. In this case, like ancient initiation rituals, it's about the death of a certain way of being. It's a death as in "death and rebirth" as opposed to death as "the end."

The Destroyer leads us through the grieving process as we acknowledge ways of being that are coming to an end. Some of this is because of the bodily processes of menopause. Eventually you can't have a baby, so there is an awareness of life being finite. Many women are either facing empty nest or letting go of the hope for a child. But there is also an attendant spiritual urge to say good-bye to life as you have known it and move on. This may take the form of allowing your children to truly grow up, or changing your work, or simply saying good-bye to an idea that no longer applies to your life.

Women often experience a loss of some kind of physical ability during this point in their lives. During the midlife passage we may be aware of tiring more easily. This means we have to let go of trying to be all things to all people. So, the task is to prioritize and get clear about what it is we most care about doing.

The Destroyer brings grieving and a willingness to start letting go of things that need to be left behind. Being the death archetype, it's difficult and it can be as far as some people get. They have no sense of anything beyond. They see menopause as just a death, just an end. That's when people can start dying. They start closing down and getting rigid, seeing themselves as washed up. It's the danger point for the Destroyer. The danger of the Seeker archetype, by the way, is that you become so iconoclastic in searching that you no longer connect with anybody and you can't find a way back.

Many times the archetypes work in progression—one leading to the other. Like a spiral. For instance, the Lover archetype often becomes active after the Destroyer. What happens when we start letting go is that we become aware of our need for other people, our need for connection. Sometimes the Destroyer archetype comes as a catastrophe, like the loss of a child or business or loved one, or perhaps serious health problems. Afterward, that sense of needing other people becomes very strong.

If you think about children's books like *Pinocchio* or *The Velveteen Rabbit* that concern the process of becoming real—which is what any of these passages are about—almost always there is some process of loss and suffering, and some process of real love. Not clinging, and not dependent, but *real* reciprocal love.

In times of transition, the Lover can become the link between the Destroyer and the Creator. As we let go, we die to one thing and get reborn. The Lover provides a sustaining function. What is it that we cherish and want to keep? What is it that we want to connect to?

The Lover is even related to the simplifying urge I talked about. Who are the people you really love? What are the places you really love? What are the activities that satisfy you?

The Lover is also the follower of bliss and is what impels people to do the things that they love. But it's also about connections. Sometimes when the Lover emerges, it means disconnecting from what you have loved and reconnecting to new things that now satisfy you more. Or it can be reconnecting to old things in a new way.

The Lover archetype starts transforming the experience of letting go from a problem into an opportunity. The Destroyer archetype is the creator of space because it takes away all our superficiality. It's also about deepening. And, of course, the more authentic and the closer to your core you are, the deeper your love can be and the greater intimacy you can have.

Remember in *The Velveteen Rabbit* when the rabbit became real? The rabbit became real only after he was all beat up and had lost one eye. One of the great opportunities in losing some conventional attractiveness is that you begin to know that people love you for you.

So after you've become the Velveteen Rabbit, after you've moved out of Caregiver, passed through the Destroyer, and welcomed the Lover into your life, you can expect the Creator archetype to present itself.

The Creator archetype is about creating a new life for yourself that fits the new transformed you who's gone through this kind of passage. A friend of mine who was experiencing an even later passage—she was sixty-five and going into retirement—told me that she was going into therapy. She didn't have any problems, she said, but she wanted a life that was hand-crafted, not mass-produced. Her passage was about how to create a life that fit, that wasn't pre-programmed.

That's the task that needs to come out of this passage. Menopausal women should ask themselves: Now that I've given up and grieved and recommitted to people and places and activities and started to fall in love with some new ones, what kind of life can I put together?

HELP FROM THE MAGICIAN

Each of us has a hand in creating our own lives. Once we are willing to assume responsibility for co-creation rather than assigning our destiny to some outside, other-than-self power, new avenues unfold and we can begin to change things seemingly unchangeable. Enter the realm of the old woman.

During the course of our conversation, I asked Dr. Pearson to address the subject of conscious co-creation. Because of my visitation, I believe that menopausal women have special access to the Magician archetype. I believe our power to consciously co-create increases with age. Here is what Dr. Pearson said.

I've always had a sense of spiritual connectedness, but it seems more complicated these days than it used to. It feels to me that there is some kind of divine presence that is creating my life and I'm creat- ✓ ing my life because I'm part of that, but you are also creating my life because you're in the room with me and we are connected with each other. The more I read about modern science, the clearer it is to me that people are not as separate as we tend to act. So that sense of creation is, in fact, a cooperative venture.

I am also very aware that we are, in fact, creating our own lives. There are ways that our lives change by simply reframing what is happening to us. For example, we all go through some of the same things. There is menopause. There is death. We don't necessarily individually create those. It's part of what it means to be a woman on the earth at this time and to be in a body. But we do have choices.

Magic begins to happen when we stop fighting life or trying to manipulate or control it. Magic is fostered by radical trust in the universe and our own choices.

Menopause can be thought of as a great tragedy—your life is over and you are no longer worth anything—or it can be a transition, an initiation into a deeper way of living. The choice of which it is depends largely on what we think it is, because both could be true. Magicians typically reframe experiences in ways that expand consciousness and allow room for grace.

Menopausal symptoms, like those of puberty, demand that we pay attention to the body. If we name our experience as "falling apart," we inadvertently are guilty of evil sorcery—that is, naming our own experiences in a way that constricts life. The positive Magician has another option: to trust the process and be open to learning what it means. In many magical traditions "dismemberment" occurs in an initiatory trance or vision. For magical women, the coming apart of former ways of being initiates us into expanded powers.

As we move through the initiation of menopause we can reclaim the wisdom of the body—the bones, the womb. Post-menopausal wisdom is whole body wisdom. Like the Oracles of the past, when we enter this place of mind/body oneness, miracles occur. We come to understand that everything we experience and do matters if we allow it to change us. As we are changed, ripple effects occur that affect all the systems of which we are a part—our families, our friends, our workplaces, and the society in which we live.

We all need to be open. I don't want to limit what I think is true based on my own personal level of consciousness. It may be somebody else can do things I can't do. We are just beginning to understand the whole idea of miracles and the fact that they are real and everyday. The more we get that, the more surprises there may be in terms of what's possible.

THE PITFALLS

As we venture *consciously* into this little-known territory of magic and menopausal wisdom, there are pitfalls. There are monsters who can snare us in their jaws.

One pitfall comes through underestimating or overestimating the experience. The equivalent is mothering. Some people act as if they didn't have kids and neglect their children, and other people get so obsessed with mothering that their child is smothered. My sense is that you can get overly involved with every hot flash and feeling and let it take you over, or you can ignore it. Either one misses the point.

Overly dramatizing and denying are part of the same thing. Having an appropriate consciousness about a passage, whether it's menopause or death or marriage or divorce, is what we're after.

Another pitfall accompanies the physical changes we experience. Any time there are major chemical changes in the body, you have feelings that are mainly related to those chemical changes. So there is also a danger of getting lost in those feelings and making judgments or decisions about your life based on feelings that are simply a result of hormones changing.

We need to have a consciousness that can allow us to have these strong emotional feelings without being overly identified with them. Women need to develop a part of themselves that can watch and have an independent judgment. It is something similar to a meditative consciousness, a sense of self that is separate from the feelings that self is having. We need to be able to say "I am experiencing this process, which is a process that all women on the planet experience, and it is not personal." If you can differentiate between yourself and your emotions, then it's less likely that you will be *controlled* by your feelings.

It's a lot like puberty, except we are wiser. One of the great opportunities is to learn to have the feelings and to learn from the feelings without having them take us over, which means not to block them, not to repress them, not even to transcend them, but to have them and have them fully.

HEALING IMAGES OF SELF AND OTHERS

Menopausal women should expect to have strong feelings arise, and learning to deal with these feelings, no matter what they are about, is the growth opportunity. This is especially true in terms of our self-image.

Many women have internalized the old cultural ideas that they are worthless if they can no longer have children and that they are less physically attractive. But postmenopausal women are getting better and better looking. This tells us something about the stereotype. Women used to look older because their opportunities were shutting down, and so they felt despair and unhappiness. But that doesn't have to be. Today, women's opportunities are expanding.

Yet there are still women who feel that no one will love them, and the belief system that you are no longer attractive begins to be a self-fulfilling prophecy. I have noticed that some women at midlife start disappearing. They feel they're not worth anything, so they don't take up any space so they don't get any attention. And the less attention they get, the worse they feel about themselves. It's a self-defeating spiral downward. But I think there are enough examples now of self-actualized postmenopausal women who are doing wonderful things with their lives, who are vital, who look terrific, and who have put their lives together in a variety of ways— with men, with women, or alone. If women will simply notice and start paying attention and making lists of positive role models, they can begin to identify with those possibilities rather than the more negative stereotypes.

For instance, one woman came to me with the idea that she didn't have love in her life and that she wanted love. She was a postmenopausal woman who was living alone and who wanted a primary relationship because she felt lonely. The first thing I had her do was make a list of all the people who loved her and who she loved. She came back and said, "I don't need a primary relationship—I have plenty of love."

We should notice how many women there are who are great role models. Once we do this, we can begin to say, "Oh, I'd like to be like her." This will increase our choices. For instance, right now there's a Unity minister downtown named Amelie Frank. She's eighty-four years old and just took on responsibilities as the minister of the new church. She's totally in charge of that church, radiates energy and joy, and has a wonderful time all the time, as far as I can tell. So I put her on my list.

I used to notice women who were career women like me. But now I'm also noticing women who've had a much more conventional life, but who have a clear sense of who they are—homemakers who are clearly not making decisions based on what other people think but on what fulfills them—and adding them to my list. I am now able to see how happy they are.

It doesn't seem to be the life you picked that makes a difference, but the fact that you picked. And even if you didn't consciously know that you were making a choice, what makes the difference is to come to terms with the fact that, on some level, you *did* choose.

Lists can help in making peace with one's choices. They can prompt us to understand why, on an underlying level, we might have chosen what we did. Let's say you chose to marry somebody who was not so great. But you learned tolerance and independence, to live your own life. You can see that there are many things you got out of making what seemed to be an unfortunate choice.

This is a tool that women can use to move away from feeling regret and toward viewing life in a more "magical" way, to rename experiences in positive ways and see what forces were at work to teach what lessons.

MENOPAUSAL MAGIC

Some years ago when I used to do workshops with Anne Wilson Schaef, there was a *curandera,* a Mexican healing woman, and she talked to us about PMS. She said the reason Anglos had PMS was that they didn't know it was the time of magic. If you knew it was the time to do magic and the time of power, you could use the power to change things and then you wouldn't have the PMS symptoms.

I thought that was interesting and meditated on it. I realized that in terms of "singing with the moon" in that premenstrual period, the magic that made the most sense to do was a conscious letting go. I also realized that postmenstruation energy is congruent with invoking. I told my clients and friends about this, and now there are a fair number of women who've developed a monthly ritual of letting go and then invocation. Every month during that time they are essentially in a ritualistic state of a passage, and it seems to work wonderfully for them in terms of letting go of habits or people or whatever it is that needs to go in their life.

I think menopause is just a bigger version of this monthly ritual. But the journey it calls us to take is different. Part of the challenge of the menstruating years is to get in alignment and see
yourself as in the fertility cycle of death and rebirth. Menopause
challenges us to align to its own realm, which I believe is in the
universe and consciousness of art.

Recently I was leading a guided fantasy and—this has never
happened to me before—I got pulled into it. I had to say, "You will
have a few minutes without the sound of my voice," meaning, I'm
going under folks; I'll be back in a few minutes for you.

The fantasy was about Dionysus and Apollo. Afterward, I realized that it probably had something to do with menopause. I had
visualized moving out of the life cycle primarily defined by natural
death and rebirth patterns (Dionysus)[6] and into the world of the
gods who can change form to create beauty (Apollo).[7] Similarly,
when we make the menopausal passage, we are leaving behind the
time in our lives when we are concerned with life and death on a
physical level, and entering a period when our concerns turn toward *creating* things that transcend life and death.

For some people, the creation of art is about immortality, but I
don't mean that in a "build the building in my honor with my
name on it" way. One of my favorite characters in all of literature
is Mrs. Ramsey from Virginia Woolf's book *To the Lighthouse.* Mrs.
Ramsey is a traditional postmenopausal woman. Her husband is a
philosopher and quite the egocentric.

The Ramseys are both having postmidlife immortality issues.
Mr. Ramsey wants to become immortal by writing the great book

[6]According to *Bulfinch's Complete Mythology* (Spring Books, Great Britain, 1964,
page 11), Dionysus (or Bacchus) is the son of Jupiter and Semele and was considered a god of fertility.
[7]From the *Standard Dictionary of Folklore, Mythology and Legend,* Harper & Row,
San Francisco, 1972. Apollo is one of the most important Greek gods. He represents youth, beauty, poetry, music, and the wisdom of oracles.

that will always be remembered. But what Mrs. Ramsey does is interesting. Mrs. Ramsey's great work is transient, a dinner party. She realizes that what she has at her party is a lot of separate egos. She chats and does some things and then she has some children light the candles. She's really doing an informal ritual—even though it just appears to be a dinner party—in which suddenly everyone becomes one together.

Virginia Woolf says that it is in such moments that we touch eternity. But it's a different kind of immortality. It's not that you are going to live on or everybody is going to know who you were, but that you are creating moments and creating experiences in which people touch the eternal, the immortal.

That's what art is about, whether it is the art of a dinner party or a wonderful quilt or something that's going to be in a library or hung on a wall someday. It is moving out of the world of all the fertility gods and the cyclical world of time, and into the realm of touching the eternal.

I believe this is what the second half of life is about.

ON THE SUBJECT OF MEN

Men have menopause, too—they just don't have the physical symptoms. *Ms* magazine had an article some years ago stating that men experienced hormonal changes similar to women's. I don't know the details, but I do know that men go through midlife crisis that, while not the same, is similar. The chief difference is that they can continue to have children, should they want to.

However, it's more permissible for a man to escape the aging crisis by finding a younger woman than for a woman to escape the crisis by finding a younger man. There are also more available younger women willing to do it. But there are an awful lot of men who do not want to escape life, who want to experience deepening initiations and who appreciate the fact that they have a woman with some maturity and experience to be with. So I don't think that it's hope-less. There's not much a woman can do if she is involved with a man who really wants to escape his own crisis with a younger woman, ex-cept she can understand that it is an anima attack and it's not per-sonal. If you understand that, it doesn't have to be so devastating.

Look at how many happy marriages there are. It happens all the time, if you look around. Men are hungering at midlife to be loved for themselves and to be known for themselves. Maybe somebody who's twenty can admire them for their power and their money, but she's not going to know them in the same way as their wife does.

The other piece is, of course, that men have the same hunger women have—to know that they are loved even when they're not perfect and when they're not powerful and when they are not in charge. There's no one else who can replace that. If you have his-tory, you've got a lot going. If you are willing to help the man con-nect with his soul as you connect with yours, then I think there can be a deepening of the relationship.

Curiously, I've noticed that men like me better than they used to. I don't look as good as I once did, but they like me better. I think the reason that men like me more is that I like them more. I dealt with most of my anger during an earlier stage in life, so I'm not walking around resenting my male counterparts these days. Consequently, I'm much nicer to them and don't feel as threatened. So, men are nicer to me.

Midlife can be a Mecca with men. After midlife, women are not usually responded to as objects. Real friendship between the sexes becomes easier.

TRANSFORMING YOUR STORY

I believe that major and transformative change happens in people's lives quite easily. Many esoteric paths suggest it's hard to connect with your soul. You have to do real hard things and follow the rules of the guru. But the reality is that our souls are always wanting to speak to us and if we give an opening, they will speak.

You can doodle and look at the picture. You can talk gibberish and translate it. You can move for ten minutes and recognize what images were moving through your body. Our souls are saying: Please, please listen to me. If we just give any kind of space at all, we can hear.

Menopause asks us to listen.

You might know someone who is depressed or you might be depressed yourself. Well, depression is the unconscious energy. But don't be put off by it. James Hillman says one of the greatest things we can do is to allow ourselves to be depressed because that's how we connect to our souls.

Each person is different, but I might suggest that a woman who is experiencing depression read something like *Descent of the Goddess*. It's the story about the great goddess of the sky going under, losing everything. They take her clothes, her body, her life, and she's reborn.

Often the pull to go down (into the unconscious) is the Destroyer archetype speaking. Following this call involves seeing what needs to be sacrificed and what needs to be let go of in order for life to go on. Most of the times, our dreams and our guided fantasies will tell us where to go. I suggest in workshops that people keep track of their fantasies, the events of their lives, and their dreams. Then I have them make a collage in which the upper part is what's happening in life, the middle is their fantasies, and the lower part is their dream life. After you have done this, you should ask, what archetypal story is this? What myth am I living? And is this the archetypal story I am going to be living next? Because those times of depression tell you that it's either time to get out of the story you're in and move into a new story, or that you're in the right story but there's some piece of it you are not living out.

Sometimes we can't leave the story we are in because we aren't done with it. To that effect, events repeat themselves. That's why certain situations or people can have such a powerful presence.

Doing this kind of collage can help you see. What story am I living? Whose story is it? Am I finished with this? What do I need to do to complete it? In dreams or fantasies or guided fantasies you might begin to get images like mine of Apollo or Aphrodite. You just get an image of what's next. But this next step won't be fleshed out in a concrete way. It will just be suggested as a symbol or metaphor.

I did my own collage and discovered that I was living the story of Demeter.[8] Demeter is the story about why we have winter. It's also about the cycles of the seasons and sacrifice. In my life, I was living Demeter and dreaming Persephone, so the whole myth was active. People who have done this have often found that there's a character in a myth that they are dreaming while they are living someone else. You've got all the characters of the story in you. Some of them are being carried in your conscious life, and some are being carried in your unconscious life, and some of them are being carried by the people in your life.

For me, it was important to realize that after Demeter got Persephone back, she founded the Eleusinian mysteries.[9] These mysteries show us how to integrate the Mother/Daughter arche-

---

[8]According to *Bulfinch's Complete Mythology,* Demeter (also known as Ceres) was the daughter of Saturn and Rhea. She had a daughter named Perserpine (also known as Persephone) who became the wife of Pluto and queen of the realm of the dead or underworld. The book states, "There can be little doubt of this story of Ceres (Demeter) and Perserpine (Persephone) being an allegory. Perserpine signifies the seed-corn, which when cast into the ground lies there concealed—that is, she is carried off by the god of the underworld. It reappears—that is, Perserpine is restored to her mother. Spring leads her back to the light of day."
[9]According to *Bulfinch's Mythology,* the worship of the goddess was established under the name of the Eleusinian mysteries.

type in a way that also acknowledges and honors the masculine and releases spiritual authority. The result of knowing I was living the myth of Demeter, Persephone, and Hades led me to do more ritual and take more seriously my role as a spiritual teacher and ritualist.

Another example would be that if things are not going well with the men in your life, it could mean that there's an unresolved issue with your masculine, or with your masculine and your feminine getting connected. When that gets taken care of in your internal story, then better relationships follow in the external story.

ADVICE FOR THE PASSAGE

Oddly enough, my final advice for the menopausal passage comes from a male myth about Perceval. When Joseph Campbell talks about the Perceval myth, he talks about Perceval healing the Wounded King of the wasteland kingdom. Perceval was supposed to be able to do it spontaneously and innocently, but he fails. Then later on in life he goes back and asks the magical questions he was supposed to ask and the king is healed. Campbell says, "Well, how could that happen? It was supposed to happen only if he did it spontaneously and innocently." And Campbell concludes that with enough courage and nobility it's possible to change the laws of the gods.

What struck me is that we are living in a time between two eras, when the old ways are passing, and that this is the time when we are changing the laws of the gods. It's not only that we are living the great stories but we are *changing* the great stories. It wasn't that long ago that many women did not live long enough to experience the Red Moon Passage. So we are talking about something that is an evolutionary leap, both in the sense of longevity and in the sense of redefining what this new opportunity means.

Remember the *curandera*. If every single time you menstruate is a time of power, surely menopause is a time of incredible power. One of the ways we can use that power and energy is to create, consciously, what our lives are going to be, not only for ourselves but also for other women and the women who come after us.

We don't yet have all the new stories for this. In fact, even in these remarks I have had to borrow from male stories. However, we, as women, do not have to see the lack of stories as a definition that there is no place for us. Instead, we can rise to opportunity for creation. In my lifetime we have redefined the first half of life with the birth of feminism. The second half is a tabula rasa, in the sense that we, as women, still need to create it. We can generate the stories that will make meaning for what it's going to be for the next few generations for women, for this next era.

And this is an extraordinary point of power—where magic can occur.

PART TWO

Celebrating

"Grandmother Time"

There once was a small bird who was surrounded by darkness. The young bird was terrified of the dark and flew as fast as he could trying to escape. He flew left and right and up and down, but no matter which direction he went, it was still dark. He cried out for help, but none came. He flew faster and higher, but the darkness seemed to have no end. Finally, he could fly no longer and fell to the ground in an exhausted, painful heap. There is nothing I can do, he wept. I cannot escape the dark. And with that, the small bird fell asleep.

Later, the sun rose of its own accord.

Would that I were, but I am not the author of this parable. It was given to me years ago in a shamanic journey. At the time, I was angry and frustrated with my circumstances and yearned to change my life. In taking an inner journey to the "other side," I hoped to be blessed with a magic formula for change or to learn the steps of some sacred transformation ceremony. Miserable, longing for any morsel of hope the greater powers could give me, I closed my eyes, quieted my mind, stepped through the invisible door, and whispered, "Help."

Instead of magic—or so I thought—I was shown this story.

When I sat down to write *Red Moon Passage,* the parable once again filled my consciousness. In so many ways, we are that panicked little bird who flew and flew, trying to escape the night. We fear menopause. We fear death. We fret and stew and run in circles performing meaningless actions that have no real effect, constantly trying to escape the inescapable. All the while, time marches on. The years pass. Then, one day we give up, humbled by our lack of power to change that which cannot be changed. We look in the mirror and finally admit to ourselves and to the world that we are growing older.

Oddly enough, after we accept our circumstances, the sun rises over the horizon. Fortunes change and new reasons for happiness enter our lives.

I have watched this particular phenomenon occur in many different types of circumstances. The outward setting and who is involved don't seem to matter. But rather, it is when the ego is set aside and we *completely submit to experiencing exactly what we are experiencing* that our lives magically open to the creative flow again. I have also noticed that this is often the time when miracles occur. It is the point where we find the water we've been thirsting for or the lost cloak we've needed to keep ourselves warm.

It was after such a "giving up" that I met Kutenai.

Kachinas Kutenai is a full-blooded Apache Indian. As if to herald the unusual life that would follow, her entrance into this world was both tragic and miraculous. On January 21, 1935, on the Gila River reservation in Arizona, her father's car skidded on a patch of black ice and crashed. Both her parents died in that accident but Kutenai, who was not yet born and still in her mother's womb, was rescued.

And so began Kutenai's journey as a human being.

Kutenai lived with her maternal grandmother for most of her childhood. Although blind, her grandmother practiced tribal medicine and lived according to the ways of Apache medicine people, which is how Kutenai came to be taught the ancient traditions. As a young child under her grandmother's care, she witnessed many

traditional Indian healings. Then, as Kutenai grew older, her grandmother showed her how to recognize the different herbs by taste
and smell and taught her how to cure a variety of illnesses, both
physical and emotional, using sweat lodges, herbs, and sacred
chants.

But instead of following the path of her ancestors as her grandmother hoped, when Kutenai came of age she left the reservation
and went to college to study nursing education. During her junior
year, she enlisted in the U.S. Army and after graduation began a career as an army nurse. This was *real* medicine, she proudly told her
Apache relatives.

But years of hospital practice opened her eyes, and the lure of
the "white man's way" faded. Kutenai slowly began to realize how
wise her old, blind grandmother had actually been.

In 1965, after a heart attack, Kutenai returned to the Gila reservation and to the roots of her life. Although she continued working as a nurse, she started augmenting her practice with the Apache
ways. Soon she was healing with herbs, chants, prayer, and sweats as
well as IV solutions. In 1983 she left nursing altogether to practice
full time as an Apache medicine woman. The circle was complete.

In April 1992, I visited Kutenai in her home in San Diego, and
asked her for traditional Apache insight into the menopausal phenomenon. As we sat in her study—a small room containing two
comfortable overstuffed chairs, a desk, a floor lamp, and numerous
Native American artifacts—she shared a few of her favorite possessions. Sage smoldered in a smudge pot. An eagle feather hung on
the wall above her head. On one level the room was very small, but
for whatever reason, I had the distinct feeling that it was much
larger than the walls led me to believe.

As I looked into Kutenai's deep brown eyes, I saw many things:
tall grass blowing in the wind, a fire, a buffalo robe, a soaring eagle.
Clear, cold water flowed down the side of a mountain. I saw a wide
blue sky. A blazing sun. A piece of turquoise. Her pupils sparkled

and briefly, fleetingly, a circle of ancient ones danced to the sacred drums.

Enthralled, I looked again, but simply saw brown eyes.

Kutenai is no stranger to menopause. She experienced the transition after a hysterectomy in 1974 and has now worked with numerous women to help them successfully complete the passage into what she calls "Grandmother Time." I wanted Kutenai to tell me about this Grandmother Time, but she shook her head and said she had to begin at the beginning. "In order to understand spring, a person must know winter and summer. To understand menopause, you must understand fertility. And to understand fertility," she told me as she crossed her arms and settled back in her chair, "you should dance the Sunrise Dance."

At first I felt disappointed that she wanted to talk about fertility when I wanted to discuss menopause. But as Kutenai spoke, I began to realize that the two states of being are connected in ways I was only beginning to fathom and that for many women, making the Red Moon Passage would also involve coming to terms with fertility in a new way.

What follows is the conversation Kutenai and I had the day that I learned to honor Changing Woman and how to see the world through the eyes of an eagle.

≋ *Kachinas Kutenai* ≋

In the Apache tradition, when a young girl comes of age and begins
to bleed, she is welcomed into womanhood by her entire tribe. Her
new fertility is an occasion for great joy and will be celebrated as
such. Emergence into womanhood is too important an event to let
pass unnoticed or barely acknowledged.

The Apache Becoming-a-Woman ceremony begins by re-
questing that your godmother, or another female of stature in the
tribe, stand with you during the four days of celebration. The request is made by placing an eagle feather at your godmother's door.
If the godmother accepts, then she is agreeing to instruct you in becoming a woman.

You begin to fast. Your godmother teaches you that you have
started to bleed because you are now going to be a giver of life. It
is a proud time. A special dress is made for you. Then your godmother shows you the ways of the ceremony and teaches you the
steps of the dance.

The Sunrise Dance was born from the legends of Changing
Woman,[1] the ancient female ancestor who survived the great flood
in an abalone shell to become the first Apache. After surviving the
flood, Changing Woman was impregnated by the sun and gave
birth to Monster Slayer, who in turn killed all the monsters and

---

[1] Kachinas Kutenai, verbal, San Diego, 1992.

Itule, Bruce D. "Growing Up Apache," *Arizona Highways,* September 1992.

Allen, Paula Gunn. *Grandmothers of the Light,* Beacon Press, Boston, 1991, pages
71–83.

Locke, Raymond Friday. *Sweet Salt: Navajo Folktales and Mythology,* Roundtable
Publishing, Santa Monica, 1990, pages 145–183.

made earth habitable. According to our tradition, this is how the Apache Nation was born.

Each girl entering puberty dances to become Changing Woman, the proud giver of all life. First you dance alone. You absorb the power of the drumming and the chants. It makes you strong. Then you are given an abalone shell to go over your third eye.[2] This shell is to remind you that life is always changing. You aren't supposed to get so set in your ways that you can't make a 180-degree change. You shouldn't be so rigid that you can't evolve.

Changing Woman was so named because of her ability to transform from a young girl into an old woman and back into a young girl again. She could be one with her sister, White Shell Woman, or she could be a separate being. We should learn from these old stories. The universe is always and forever changing, so the ability to change is a good skill to have.

Now, during the dance, the young girl runs in the four directions while the community runs behind her. They do this to express their desire that the girl live through the four stages of life.[3] It is the same type of expression and comes from the same beliefs that prompted ancient hunters to dance a hunting dance and *mimic the desired kill* before setting forth. It is powerful medicine. The ceremonial running is *a reenactment of that which will come to pass in the future.*

The tribe throws cornmeal, the substance of life, and sacred cattail pollen over the girl's head. The wish is that she prosper, be

[2] According to the *Dictionary of Mysticism and the Occult,* compiled by Nevill Drury, the third eye is the sixth of the seven chakras in Kundalini yoga and is located slightly above the eyebrows at the center of the forehead. To some, it is regarded as the seat of psychic and paranormal powers.
[3] The four stages of life align with the four directions—east, south, west, and north—and represent different stages of physical and psychic growth. This concept is discussed in detail in the interview with Paula Gunn Allen (Part Five).

fertile, and live a full life. In return, the girl, acting as Changing Woman, blesses the tribe: I give you life.

Both dancing and fasting continue throughout the four days. When you fast you have visions about your future life. I remember that I saw clearly that I would bear two children. A boy and a girl.

You are also given a walking stick. There is no connotation here of growing old or being debilitated. The stick will absorb the power of the ceremony and later in life it will offer you strength. When you climb mountains or cross rivers, as you walk, from time to time you need something to steady you and help you climb. This walking stick is what you give to your offspring. This is what is passed. I am sorry that every culture doesn't have such a ceremony. It's a beautiful thing. When you greet a period in your life this way, there is something different about you afterward.

EMPOWERMENT

By becoming a woman, an Apache female is empowered. She is taught that she is a giver of all life and that this ability is respected and revered by her entire tribe. Feminine powers of fluidity, fertility, strength, and vision are ceremonially bestowed. *All* of womanhood is honored, from the powerful, ancient deity Changing Woman who gave birth to the first Apache to the thirteen-year-old mortal who is just starting to menstruate. After four days of celebration, any young girl would be hard pressed to forget the value of her role. A deep impression has been made. This is quite different from being secretive and shy and calling your new fertility the curse as so many white women say.

American women complain about having periods, and expound on what a nuisance it is. Can you see the inherent negativity? *Curse?* Rather than respect for life, there is disrespect. Rather than empowerment, there is suffering. Instead of celebrating the natural, you have taught yourselves to abhor it, to be diminished by it.

I think you white women have a lot to learn.

The transition from fertility to menopause is no different than the transition of puberty. It is a natural part of life that should be honored and celebrated. Traditional Apaches don't fear menopause. Why should they? What is there to fear? Life is life and certain things are part of life no matter what we do. By resisting what is, we create problems.

ACCEPTING LIFE AND DEATH

In the Changing Woman story, the Hero Twins, Changing Woman's children, encounter death in their travels. However, rather than slaying this monster, they let death live.

The next morning he set out northward, and travelled until he came to a place where he saw an old woman who came slowly toward him, leaning on a staff. Her back was bent, her hair was white and her face was deeply wrinkled. He knew this must be Old Age. When they met he said, "Grandmother, I have come on a cruel errand. I have come to slay you."

"Why would you slay me?" she asked in a feeble voice. "I have never harmed anyone. I hear that you have done great deeds in order that men might increase on earth, but if you kill me there will be no increase of men. The boys will not grow up to be fathers, the worthless old men will not die and The People will stand still. It is well that people should grow old and pass away and give their places to the young. Let me live and I shall increase The People."

"Grandmother, if you keep your promise I shall spare your life," said the Hero Twin, and he returned home without a trophy.[4]

In the tradition of this wisdom, Kutenai spoke to me about our fear of death.

I think American women's actions clearly say there is a resentment of growing older and on some subconscious level, a fear of death. But you should accept growing older. You should enter old age with grace and dignity. Death is on the agenda for us all.

The quest for eternal life in physical bodies seems to be a misguided urge that particularly afflicts the Caucasian race. We've all heard that women from other cultures don't experience the problems with menopause that Americans do. If you aren't afraid of what is natural, of growing older or of dying, if you don't think of aging as something "bad," then menopause won't hold the same dreaded significance.

However, things aren't that way anymore. Black women, Asian women, Hispanic women, Indian women—they didn't used to have problems with menopause, but now it's across the boards. You see, it's acceptance of what you are exposed to. We've all been acculturated.

THE POWERS OF THE WEST

As Kutenai spoke, I kept thinking of the legend of Changing Woman. After the monsters that plagued the earth had been slain, making it possible for human beings to survive, and after her children had begun having children, Changing Woman left her tribe on earth and went to live in the West with her husband, the Sun. From this new home, she comforts her husband

[4]Locke, *Sweet Salt*, page 182.

and watches over her people. She makes this change thoughtfully, feeling sad that she is leaving her children, but knowing that the time has come. Of particular note is that Changing Woman deliberated over what she would need in her new home and then asked the Sun to provide it. Only when this was done, did she move.

> *At the end of four days Changing Woman went to the top of Ch'oolii and met the Sun, who asked her to come live with him in the West. She agreed on the conditions that he would build her a house as beautiful as the one he had in the East, which her sons had told her about. "I want it built floating on the western water," she said, "away from the shore so that in the future, when people increase, they will not annoy me with too many visits. I want all sorts of gems—white shell, turquoise, haliotis, jet, soapstone, agate, and redstone—planted around my house, so that they will grow and increase. Then I shall be lonely over there and shall want something to do, for my sons and my sister will not go with me. Give me animals to take along. Do all this for me and I shall go with you to the West."[5]*

What is this new stage? I asked Kutenai. What is it that Changing Woman needed and what should we be celebrating when we move to the West?

This new stage we enter when we "move to the West," this time of life we should be celebrating, is about increased wisdom. The Apaches believe that as traditional women grow older their spiritual powers increase. It's important that women understand this and use this time of their lives and these powers correctly. A young girl is shown many wonderful feminine attributes in the Becoming-a-Woman ceremony. During her life she works to foster these attri-

[5] Locke, *Sweet Salt*, pages 179–180.

butes. After menopause, she loses her ability to be the giver of life in the form of human birth. But is this bad?

Only if one can't experience change.

Grandmother Time has its own gifts and a woman in touch with herself will continue to be a giver of life, just on a different level. She will have increased power and increased vision. But I don't mean that all women will experience this. I mean traditional women. I mean women who are following the old ways. You can't expect to have spiritual powers if you are an alcoholic or on drugs. You have to be living your life correctly.

If you are living correctly, then as you grow older the power of your prayer increases. Your period has stopped but your force has increased. That's why the role of the grandmother should be one of guidance. It should be one of advice and prayer.

Part of the reason for this increased power is that there is a decrease in sexual desire when you come into Grandmother Time. You are finally able to put sex into its proper perspective. You don't need to have an orgasm to smile and your conversation is no longer filled with sex. I know a lot of women . . . it's incredible what we will put up with and how we allow ourselves to be dominated with sex. I have to laugh when I think about how many of us put up with encounters that weren't even worth it. That's why I am teaching now that a half loaf of bread is *not* necessarily better than none.

When you stop being dominated by sexuality, when you stop being controlled by it, you view things differently. This is part of the change that happens naturally as you grow older. If we let it, that is.

Magazine articles, television shows, friends, lovers, family— American culture reinforces the sexual ideal as the pinnacle of success, even for older women who have gone through menopause. The "sexy grandmother" is promoted as being something worthy to strive for. I believe this emphasis is harmful. Growing old with dignity and grace should be our goal, and we should attempt to more knowingly embrace this wisdom. Some American women want to dye their hair and have liposuction—all these things are presented to the public as normal. But we know in our heart of hearts that they are not normal. We know that they are unsettling to our spirit. So you have to be strong.

The New Spiritual Man and Woman

White women have taught people to fear old age. It's passed on from mother to daughter, from generation to generation. So now we have to be reeducated. There has to be a reeducating and a recreating of both men and women.

A man who is wise and understands the ways of the universe wouldn't force his wife to forever look like the teenager he married, but instead he would value the power of her prayer and of her increased intuitiveness. Such a man would compliment his wife on her gray hair instead of suggesting that she dye it.

We—men and women—are in this together and in order to have a healthy society, both sexes must be strong and wise and live by the truth. I call such people the new spiritual man and the new spiritual woman. And this is some of what my practice is about—teaching people, reeducating them to become the new man and the new woman.

Our Physical Health Is a Spiritual Concern

Years as an army nurse opened my eyes to many things, but one of the most disconcerting was the medical field's attitude about benefits versus risk. The medical profession operates on a very sick concept that says that the benefits of a drug or the benefits of a surgery outweigh the risk of the drug or surgery. It has not always been this way. Doctors take an oath to "above all, do no harm." Yet somewhere in the evolution of modern medicine, it became acceptable to do harm if the doctor was also doing good. On the other hand, a medicine person, a spiritual person, cannot accept the medical premise that the benefits outweigh the risks. There is no risk involved in any treatment I do.

Every woman who's ever been told she needs to have a hysterectomy should look at some of the alternatives to surgery. If the surgery is being recommended because of fibroids, herbs like red clover and don quai can be taken.

There are many natural approaches. Herbal therapy, visualization, meditation, acupuncture, and acupressure. You should see whether you can get a reduction in the size of the fibroid first. Once the body starts to respond with reduction, you know you are on the right track. And a woman is not going to fall apart in the time that she attempts to use a natural approach.

But I don't tell people not to go to the doctor. What I do is to encourage them to get a second and third opinion before agreeing to any surgery, and I encourage them to also try natural treatments.

Mine is not a heal-all solution. I suggest to some women that they use an herbal regime, and afterward they will call and thank me. For others, nothing changes. The regime works for some but not for others. Now the medical professions say the same, but the difference is that I am not putting anyone at risk or suggesting anything that is life-threatening.

Women who are interested in trying natural approaches to hot flashes and other menopausal symptoms might try the following:

To ease discomforts

Black Cohosh	1 capsule 3 times a day
Red Sage	1 capsule 3 times a day
Dandelion	1 capsule 3 times a day

| Valerian Root | 1 capsule 3 times a day |
| Vitamin E | 100–200 units daily |

To control hot flashes

Don Quai	2 capsules 4 times a day
Siberian Ginseng	up to 2 capsules 4 times a day
Vitamin E	100–400 units daily
Calcium	2000 mg daily
Magnesium	400 mg daily
Calcium Phosphate	4 tablets every 4 hours

To ease constipation

| Elderberry Tea | 1 cup per day in the morning |

But any woman interested in following a more natural regime for handling the discomforts of menopause should seek out a trained practitioner in any of the natural healing arts. Working with a spiritual healer can increase the results from the treatment. In the end, however, it all comes back to why we are having so much physical trauma in the first place.

RECLAIMING OUR POWER

One of the main reasons we are now having trouble with natural occurrences like menopause and aging, with becoming this new man and woman, is that we've lost our connection with power. We forget that everything is interconnected and we forget that a balance of power between male and female is natural.

The idea that women have lost their power is not new. Much of the feminist movement is based on just that. But that's not exactly what I am referring to. I'm not talking about political clout. I'm talking about an internal power.

In order to recover our power, we need to begin with deprogramming women about the notion of God.

A woman has to dare to see God as male and female energy. And if a woman doesn't want to believe that, she should just look around her environment and she will see male and female trees, male and female deer, male and female birds. She can see that male and female everything exists. You can define God by whatever name you wish, but if this God had the wisdom to put male and female everything on the earth, then understand that universal mind is also male and female.

We Native Americans did not get into the ideology that God was male. I personally think it is very sad when that happens because it is so limiting to the minds of women. The Apache, the Navajo, the Sioux—we are matriarchal in nature. What has happened, sadly, is that our history was recorded by white men and they led people to believe that there were only *male* chiefs, only medicine *men*. But read our literature, our stories. White Painted Woman, Spider Woman, White Buffalo Woman, Changing Woman—the idea that God is male is not our history at all.

In all my teaching, I attempt to have everyone see the rationale for the restoration of the feminine balance and power. You can't put a man on the moon without a woman and you can't put a woman on the moon without a man. Yet we have gotten very far away from the inherent knowledge that a balance should exist.

A woman has to love herself. She has to accept herself as an equal member of society and she should recognize that she has special intuitive powers. But we've lost our spiritual antennae. So many women live under a cloud of inferiority. They don't believe they are as powerful as men, or are part of God.

A long time ago, among Native American people, a husband would proudly say: "I have a good woman. She sees." There was respect for elders because they could know things, they could see the future. We used to rely on dreams to tell us things. Native Americans would move their encampments, if one old reliable woman woke up and said, "I see a tornado coming."

So women should begin to document their intuitiveness and learn to respect it. I suggest to my clients that they put a quarter in a jar every time they use the words *weird* or *strange* to describe the intuitive information they receive. They should put a coin in every time they denigrate their dreams or an out-of-the-ordinary experience that occurs. Because every time you do that you are diminishing your spiritual powers.

Americans have been taught to be logical, to ignore their spiritual side. But women must admit to having powers. I think the real recognition that you have passed into Grandmother Time is the accuracy of your vision and the accuracy of your dreams.

My practice also involves helping others through the use of my intuition and sight. I've just returned from Alaska, where I was involved in searching for a party of men who had been lost in the wilderness. When I arrived, I asked the spirit to give me images through my dreams to see whether I was even in contact with the men. That night I had a dream and I saw these two men very clearly. I drew their pictures. Later, photographs were brought to me and it was the same men, so I knew I was connected. I saw one of the men being carried on a makeshift stretcher and I knew, at that point, that they were still alive.

This skill of receiving information is what I call "listening to the spirit guides." It's an ability that can be developed by any and all of us. But to do that, we women have to start over. We have to wake up and stop our own lies. We are pretending to be weak. We are pretending to be victims. We must break the mold and stop being so subservient and fully embrace our own powers. It's the only way to restore the balance.

Where do we start? I encourage the use of prayer as a means

to bring about change in the world. But rather than saying "oh please, please, please," which infers a weak faith, that you don't really believe you are worthy, I teach people to pray by thanking in advance for their intuitive wisdom. To thank in advance for their psychic powers, that their third eye is reopened so they can hear and see. In other words, don't pray for someone else to intervene, but thank the Great Spirit for the power and wisdom to intervene yourself.

Prayer is one aspect of unleashing our inherent powers, but if a woman wants to learn to reconnect, to uncover her own abilities, she should also meditate. Meditation has a calming effect. It's a focusing. I teach a type of meditation that gives a person a spiritual sound. By repeating this spiritual sound, your spiritual body is strengthened. You begin to open.

Then you also have to visualize. It activates the creative. You should visualize whatever it is you are praying about. It's not unlike the Sunrise Dance and the tribal hunters reenacting that which will come to pass. Such acts were, and still are, powerful medicine.

LIVING IN HARMONY

Living wisely, living in harmony involves more than ancient creation secrets or visions of the future floating around inside your head. We have to understand that we are all connected. We are all brothers and sisters, and we have to stop practicing racism, sexism, and specieism. White males are not the only important people and human beings are not the only important species on this planet. That's why I also teach everybody to look at life from the eye of an eagle, from the eye of a buffalo, and from the eye of an ant. Before you act, look at any problem in this way. And if you get a yes from all the views and from the Creator's view and Mother Earth's view, then you make a decision to move forward.

If we want to live wisely, then menopausal women should gather together and honor their transition. Take the initiative. Act. They should create their own ceremonies based on their own traditions and embrace this new phase of their lives.

And above all, they should celebrate it.

PART THREE

Reclaiming Our Crown,

Becoming Crone

WHENEVER I HAVE A PROBLEM, whenever I'm searching for something or aching inside from a sadness, my first instinct is to turn to the available literature for answers. I curl up on the living room couch or close the door to my office during lunch hour and read. This is my coping mechanism. This is how I deal with life.

I believe that ideas can change reality, that as we think, we act, and so evolves the world. Consequently, ideas are the weapons and ointments and treasures I seek.

More often than not, I am rewarded for these retreats of concentration with knowledge and insight. By reading what my contemporaries have to say, I learn of new concepts and different ways of looking at life, or I learn about old ideas that have stood the test of time or, after weathering abandonment, have finally resurfaced because they are once again meaningful to the culture.

As I quested after the deeper meaning of menopause and how a woman could turn the aging process into a bountiful experience full of new life, as I sought insight into the old crone of my vision, I naturally turned to the current literature for answers. What did our feminine scholars know about the old woman as an archetype?[1] What had they discovered about the change of consciousness that

---

[1]According to C. G. Jung, archetypes are primordial types or "universal images that have existed since the remotest times."

accompanies age? And what could history and myth tell us about this period of a woman's life?

Barbara Walker was an obvious choice for mentor. She is a scholar, a historian, a feminist, and a prolific author with over twenty books to her name, including a dictionary of feminine symbols and an encyclopedia of women's myth. While others will urge that you listen to your soul, Barbara will tell you to crack open the textbooks and study the ancient goddess religions. "You can't have the consciousness if you don't know anything about it," she sternly told me.

The human race has a contiguous history that builds upon itself. The goddess myths are both our heritage and our future. They are the stories that tell us where we came from and what is possible for we who are human/divine. The process of studying these legacies from our past is not unlike being on an archeological dig. And sometimes, as with Barbara, you discover gold.

In two of her books, *The Crone: Woman of Age, Wisdom and Power,* and *The Skeptical Feminist: Discovering the Virgin, Mother and Crone,* Barbara addresses why the powerful and age-old archetype of a postmenopausal woman, that of Crone, is both loved and feared; why it has been banished from our psyches during the past 2,000 years; and why this primal image and its accompanying myths are beginning to reemerge in our modern-day world.

Her underlying theory is based on the Jungian concept of the collective unconscious, particularly the premise that there are shared emotional feelings connected to archetypal images and ideas. In a paper on the psychology of individuation, Carl Jung wrote that the psychic contents he termed "collective" included ideas as well as feelings, and that the collective unconscious of families, cultures, or humankind at large would contain intellectual concepts as well as emotional feelings regarding those concepts.[2]

[2]Jung, C. G. *The Basic Writings of C. G. Jung,* The Modern Library, New York, 1959, page 244.

In Barbara's work, the collective idea is that of Crone and the emotional feeling is fear.

Say the word *crone* and watch people, be it ever so slightly, recoil. Dropped eyes, a quick flush around a neck, a small step backward, a little finger that suddenly jerks, or a chill that raises almost imperceptible bumps on an arm—the image invoked by the word *crone* and the feelings it calls up are not pleasant. This shouldn't be surprising. Check your dictionary. *Webster's II University Dictionary* defines the word *crone* as "a witch-like old woman." *The American Heritage Dictionary* defines the word as "an ugly, withered old woman." These are not kind or loving descriptions. But it's no mistake that the words *old* and *witch* are used in tandem. While our culture no longer tortures gifted women by burning them at the stake as in days gone by, the collective unconscious shared by our society still contains the idea of crone as frightening, repulsive, and perhaps even evil.

With this image as a model, what woman in her right mind would want to grow old? Who would desire to become such a thing? Oh, we say, why has nature played such a cruel trick on us?

Barbara points out that this was not always the meaning of crone, nor was it the original significance of the old woman archetype. In ancient cultures, the archetype of the crone was that of a woman of wisdom and power. Older religions revered the Crone as the wise oracle. But in the past 2,000 years this image has been banished to our deepest psyches and a new and very limited idea, that of Crone as witch and harbinger of death, has taken hold. It's not that this idea isn't true, Barbara says, because the Crone does have those qualities, but this image is not complete. Mother Death is only one aspect of an old woman's essence.

Part of Barbara's mission is to recover the full nature of the Crone by bringing the original archetype into the light of consciousness again. To the extent that we only access part of the archetype, we are handicapped. It's like trying to sail a sloop with just

a jib. It's possible, but if we want to travel the oceans we'd best un-
furl our mainsail.

Jung explained that an archetype will take "its color from the
individual consciousness in which it happens to appear," and that it
will be "altered by being perceived."[3] This is why I find the search
for the old woman archetype so exciting. The journey here is not
merely a staid scholarly stroll through history during which we un-
earth the facts. It's a dynamic process. As we discover her true and
full essence, the archetypal idea of Crone—and our very selves
along with it—will transform.

When I started writing this book, I called Barbara on the
phone. I told her who I was and what I was doing and asked if I
could come see her. She graciously agreed. A year later, I finally arrived on her doorstep. Barbara lives in the New Jersey countryside,
in the woods by a beautiful lake. We spent the day talking, walking,
eating wild blueberries, looking at rocks, and wiggling our feet in
the sand.

This is what she said about the menopausal journey into
cronehood.

---

[3] Jung, *The Basic Writings,* pages 288–290.

≋ *Barbara G. Walker* ≋

*Out of the waters of the Ganges arose a young woman of extra-
ordinary beauty, far advanced in pregnancy. With graceful gait she
ascended the banks of the river and a few moments later gave birth
to a charming baby. She affectionately held the infant and suckled
it. Suddenly, the woman was transformed into a cruel and frightening hag. In this terrifying aspect, she seized the child, crushed it
with her grim jaws and swallowed it. She then reentered the waters of the river whence she had emerged.*[4]

LESSONS FROM KALI MA

The mental and spiritual concomitants of menopause usually include a deep-gut realization of one's own mortality. While this realization might have previously been understood intellectually, it is
seldom *felt* until the right stage of the life cycle is reached.

At first, this feeling was somewhat traumatic for me. But when
I relaxed into it with acceptance and understanding, allowing my
mind to follow where my body led, I discovered that my initial re-
luctance was imposed by cultural bias, not produced by my essential self.

This is when I became very interested in the Crone Goddess,
particularly the ancient Hindu Goddess, Kali Ma.[5] She, as the

[4]Brown, C. Mackenzie. "Kali, the Mad Mother," an essay contained within *The
Book of the Goddess, Past and Present,* Crossroads, New York, 1992. Brown quoted
this passage from *The Gospel of Sri Ramakrishna,* Ramakrishna-Vivekananda Center, New York, 1944.
[5]Kali (the black one) is an ancient Hindu goddess, most typically known for being
the goddess of destruction. However, she is also the most supreme mother goddess

Crone Goddess, represented what my inner divinity was changing into and I wanted to be comfortable with that.

Even though she is an ancient goddess, Kali still has an active working temple. I have a friend in California who goes to Calcutta every year in November to attend the Kali Puja, which is the great festival of Kali at the Dakshineswar temple. She says that thousands of people come from all over India and other places to honor Kali Ma in this temple. They look upon her as the mother of humanity, as both life giving and life taking. She's not only the ugly crone, she's also the virgin and mother aspects. She's the trinity. Kali destroys, but she also creates.

As a goddess, Kali is usually shown with four arms. In each hand she holds one of the element symbols—earth, air, fire, and water. This symbolizes that she was the creator and brought forth everything from these four elements. She wears a necklace of skulls on which is carved the letters of the Sanskrit alphabet. These letters represent the original alphabet that had the magical power to create what was spoken in that language. Kali said what was to be, and when she said it, it became true.

This kind of goddess is the foundation of all the patriarchal god stories. Later, men copied the same story and said that "God" created by speaking, that "He" made the elements and separated heaven from earth. But I discovered that ancient history says all these things were originally done by the Goddess. I think it helps women to know that, to know that these concepts were probably woman-inspired.

My research was enlightening. Kali is well known as the Goddess of Destruction. Yet if I had never heard of this death aspect of

of India. According to the *Standard Dictionary of Folklore, Mythology and Legend,* "In some tantra texts she stands on a boat floating on an ocean of blood, drinking from a skull the lifeblood of children she brings forth, then eats back."

the Goddess, of Kali as Mother Destruction and Kali as Crone, I would have had difficulty assimilating the sense of mortality that seems to accompany the menopausal experience. As I studied, I began to comprehend the deep meaning symbolized by Kali in a new way. She showed me that the darker, declining ebb tide of life is just as sacred in its own way as birth or youth. It has its own beauty, just as the barren places of earth have their own stark beauty.

Death is not a single event. It's a slow process that starts happening from birth, because Nature is continually destroying us. As we get older, more and more cells of our body and brain deteriorate and die, and this is why the skin doesn't regenerate itself as well and why our physiology gets a little less efficient. So death is happening in life.

I think of death as being a return to the cauldron, to the Crone's cauldron. Everything living is in it, all mixed up in a mush, and it comes out in different forms. Rather than thinking of an individual personality as persisting after death, my concept of the vast generalized life force is much like the American Indians' view. They look upon their ancestors as being the environment. They believe that after death, people go back into the soil, into the water, and the atmosphere. So a molecule of air that you breathe might once have been part of Cleopatra because all the matter on this earth is basically the same. It just takes different forms.

What the figure of Kali says is that destruction and creation co-exist. They are not separate. They are not the opposite poles of anything, but are always together. We live by destroying other life forms and other forms live off us when we are destroyed. It's all part of the same cauldron, part of the ongoing process all the time. When you look death in the eye this way, as do the followers of Kali Ma, you can stop being afraid of it.

Kali tells us much about creation/destruction and our role in that cycle. In my book, *The Skeptical Feminist,* I wrote,

On getting past Kali's movie monster caricature, one might find a rational statement of feminine theology (thealogy) that the patriarchal world has found convenient to forget. Her image states that what we call ugliness is essential to the world of living nature. Every flower must have its roots in organic rot. . . .

I learned to appreciate Kali's ugliness as I learned to accept the somatic facts of my own aging and eventual death. That, of course, was the whole purpose of her image. To know life clearly, one must see it all: the end as well as the beginning, the decay as well as the growth. . . . Kali's ugliness stands as a warning to those who trespass on her mysteries without proper preparation and mental acceptance. Like life, she is fatal. Like knowing the worst, she allays fear. Like wisdom, she appears to those who are not afraid. Like love, she brings regeneration out of crude organic reality.[6]

RITUALS—CONNECTING TO THE UNCONSCIOUS

The unconscious is always there, but we have been conditioned by a patriarchal society to not pay attention to what is inside ourselves, to ignore our own wisdom. We are taught from childhood that we are not as wise as the wise men. I don't believe this is true. Doctors and psychologists have very little notion of women's true vitality and intuitions and insights, so I don't think they are the "authorities" we should be looking to for knowledge about ourselves.

We have wisdom, if we would just pay attention. It's there.

[6] Walker, *The Skeptical Feminist*, pages 195–197.

I attend monthly meetings of a women's group. Many of the women who come to the Full Moon Group say things like, "I have been looking for this all my life and didn't know where to find it." Statements like this indicate that these women are meshing with this content (the study of Goddess religions) in a way that they could not do in a traditional religion or whatever it is that they have been doing before.

At the meetings we perform rituals to help us connect. We pass the talking stick and everybody has something to say. Exactly what we do depends on the season and situation because there are different rituals for each season (e.g., Beltane, Lammas, the vernal equinox, winter solstice) and there are different rituals for different purposes (e.g., honoring the earth, centering, rebirthing, learning).[7]

I am going to conduct a croning ritual for a friend who is going through menopause. First, following the way of matriarchal tribes, she will be crowned. The crown signifies that she is reaching a power stage in her life. Then she will receive gifts. I am going to make paper strips for people to write what they wish for her cronehood. We'll put these strips into a special box and present her with that. I'll also have people talk about their own attitudes about Crone and then we'll do the usual things—drumming and perhaps dancing.

I think the croning ritual is very important. Women feel better about the whole process when they see it celebrated. It's the same as celebrating a young girl's menarche. I have several friends who have held ceremonies for their daughters—they have a red party. The girls feel so much better about having periods as a result, because it's no longer shameful and hidden and dirty and disgusting and all that we were told when we were kids.

[7] Rituals to help women are detailed in *Women's Rituals* by Barbara G. Walker, Harper & Row, San Francisco, 1990.

The majority of women are intimidated by patriarchy and intimidated by their own physical deterioration, if you call it that. But matriarchal people did not consider it deterioration when women developed wrinkles and grew fatter. This was a sign of maturity rather than falling apart. We need to be told that cronehood is not dirty and disgusting and that elder women are not ugly and that we have the right to look the way we look and be the way we are. A croning ritual is one way to accomplish this.

In the ancient matriarchal societies, a woman automatically became a priestess in that elder period of her life. She was assimilated to the earth powers. In this tradition, because she was keeping her magic blood within, a woman became wise. Menstrual blood is the wise blood. The moon blood knows how to make life. So rather than something to be mourned (loss of ability to have children), cronehood in the ancient matriarchal tribes was something to be celebrated (entering the circle of the wise priestess).

We need to honor this tradition again.

GODDESS RELIGIONS AND THE CRONE

Barbara and I talked about the idea of a new religion evolving from the women's movement. My own dissatisfaction with conventional religion came from a longing to have a direct spiritual experience. In most patriarchal religions, knowing the mind of God is reserved for those in authority. Many men and most women, much less fifteen-year-old girls, are not allowed in the club. But reemerging female wisdom tells us we prosper when we dissolve the separation between God and self.

I think the consciousness that is emerging now is a result of the tremendous volume of feminine scholarship that's been going on for the past ten years. In 1983, when I published the *Woman's Encyclopedia of Myths and Secrets,* there was very little. There were no women's studies courses in universities, and there was no feminist literature to speak of except Merlin Stone's book. But in one decade it has blossomed, and some of this is filtering down to the women who have never read any of this literature, who have never thought of themselves as feminists. It's percolating through all society.

The pope is even complaining about it.

What's worrying the religious leaders is that we are actually seeing a lot of women walk out of the churches and find better spirituality in the women's groups. Why are women seeking another form of spirituality? Because in patriarchal religions, there is you, there is the priest or minister, and there is God. The priest or minister is a mediator between you and the spiritual experience. It is a hierarchy. On the other hand, the whole thrust of female spirituality is to refute the *transcendence* of a deity. The deity that women envision is always *immanent*, not transcendent. It's "in." The deity is in us and in nature. It's the life force. The deity is living things on the planet and not something outside this universe.

This is why women need to study Goddess religions. Until a woman studies the alternatives and knows what other kinds of religious concepts are out there, I don't think she can really attain her true power. She may have so much strength within that she appears strong without even thinking it, like the pioneer women who tamed the wilderness. Those were strong women. But they didn't know they were strong *in themselves* and there is a big difference between the two concepts. Those women thought their strength came from a patriarchal god or maybe they did not even think about it.

Our awareness of where our power actually comes from needs to be more conscious. The whole idea needs to be thought about. Studying the Goddesses and being involved in a Goddess religion is about the only place that you can get this sort of consciousness.

We have few valid images of the Goddess left in western civilization, except as symbols secretly hidden away. That's why it's important for us to study folklore, fairy tales, pagan mythology, and symbolic divination systems like the tarot and the I Ching, whose original versions date back to a matriarchal worldview. Properly interpreted, such systems tell us much about the mind-set of our ancestors and may contribute to a new feminine theology that might help restore balance to this world. We desperately need to return to a more sophisticated comprehension of the Crone Goddess and what she represents, which is a more love-affirming and death-accepting philosophy.

RECOVERING THE VIRGIN MARY

For instance, the Virgin Mary is a powerful female image, but not as powerful as she might be. She is the Virgin and the Mother combined, but she has no Crone. Her Crone aspect has been completely exorcised.

Mary's origins are in the ancient mythologies. She was originally the Goddess, but the church declared her "all human" and devised the doctrine of the Immaculate Conception so that she would be different from all other women, but still not a deity.

Now, you must understand that the original Goddess was a trinity. She was always the Virgin, Mother, and Crone. Then she would cycle back and become the Virgin again. Which is why in mythology Persephone, whose name means Destroyer or Crone, cycled back and became the Virgin, Kore. Then she passed into the Mother stage as Demeter.

Cyclic trinities occur in all the old mythologies, and at one point there was a Crone phase in Mary. Very early on in the Ephesus cult[8] there are three Marys and according to prevalent legend,

---

[8] Ephesus was an ancient city located on the mouth of the Cayster River, famous in antiquity for its cult dedicated to Artemis, or Diana. (From *Ephesus after Antiquity* by Clive Foss, 1980.) According to the Bible, in "The Acts of the Apostles," Acts 19–20, the city of Ephesus was the guardian of Diana's temple and of her statue that fell from heaven.

Mary lived at Ephesus in her old age.[9] The Bible tells about the three Marys standing at the foot of the cross, like the three fates standing at the foot of Odin's tree.[10] The significant idea here is that one of the three was always the death-bringer who decreed the sacrificial death of the god.

I believe this is why the image and idea of Mary as Crone was banished. As Mother Death, she is too threatening. The female principle was previously regarded as both the life-giver (Mother) and the death-bringer (Crone). But Mother Death is a power that men fear. She represents the kind of death our culture wishes to conceal, making it invisible as old women are made invisible. She represents ordinary death—death in old age, death from wasting disease, death after slow degeneration of body and mind.

But this aspect of the Goddess is reemerging. In *The Crone*, I wrote that "the secret image of the old woman as Mother Death, the Crone, once found conscious recognition everywhere because it was essential to the older religious systems. Patriarchal faiths undertook to eliminate it, laboring in ignorance of what we are just beginning to rediscover; namely, that archetypes can be suppressed but not destroyed, and their suppression can be socially catastrophic."[11]

In ancient times, when the Crone was recognized as part of the Goddess's nature, when the Crone was seen as an image that represented truth, old women were *not* regarded as useless objects. They were instead valued. The elder tribal mothers looked after the law, morality, religion, and magical lore. And this is what must be again.

[9] Branston, Brian. *Gods of the North,* Thames & Hudson, London, 1955.
[10] John 19:25. *The Jerusalem Bible*, Doubleday, New York, 1968. "Near the cross of Jesus stood his mother and his mother's sister, Mary the wife of Cleophas, and Mary of Magdala."
[11] Walker, *The Crone,* page 19.

STAYING WITH YOUR TRIBE

What's most tragic about our patriarchy is the way it has discon-
nected the old mothers and grandmothers from their families, from
their tribes. The children grow up and have their own children and
they go to live in some other place. People are moved around constantly. When corporations move, the husbands (or wives) drag the
family along. The grandmothers are back in a hometown by themselves and their children and grandchildren are not with them. This
is tragic.

The family is a natural human association. It is the way humans
in the wild behaved. And the old mothers had a leading role in the
tribe. Except for a few ethnic groups who do stay together, we've
completely lost that idea of tribalism. But it's not the natural way
for humans to live. Families need to become tribes again.

THE RESPONSIBILITIES OF CRONE

I have strong opinions about cronehood. I think elder women
should influence the moral and ethical standards of the country. I
think this is the natural way for healers to behave. The old mothers
are the ones who should set the standards, just as younger mothers
set the standards for their children growing up. I don't think you
outgrow motherhood and I think the grown children should still
listen to the older mothers.

But at the same time the mothers have to become truly wise
and not end up being wimps or doormats or dummies or people
grieving about their empty nest. They need to employ themselves.
In a way, they have to take intellectual power. It isn't given to them.
They have to make an effort to find it and take it.

The Crone is the most powerful female figure humanity has
ever known. She is the one who really scares people. And in a cer-

tain sense, I think we need to scare people. We need to get their attention. The Crone's left ("sinister") eagle eye is the one that sees through to the truth. There again, she is necessary as a threat. If you don't want the truth known, you certainly aren't going to welcome anyone who can see into your life. But we need more candor and less dissimulation in our society. So, the Crone figure, frightening though she is, ugly though she is, is necessary to women to enhance their spiritual power.

There's a lot of power in the word *no* and that's part of the power of the Crone. She's negative. She says no. If women all over the world said no, the world would change. No, I won't send my son to your war. No, I won't go to your churches and worship your god. And no, I won't let your male obstetrician deliver my daughter's child.

Our world desperately needs that wisdom. Western civilization has gone off the paths of common sense and has lost itself in a wilderness of violence, exploitation, and destruction. The elder women may be likely to have more sensible ideas about honoring and conserving life on this planet than those who currently rule. Native Americans celebrated the aging woman as an indication of help and guidance for their tribe's future generations. Until our culture can treasure its elder women for similar reasons and to learn to once again live by the perceptions and insights of the feminine experience, it will remain alienated from some of the best products of the human mind.

I believe woman wisdom, the wisdom of the Crone, may be our best hope for a livable future.

(PART FOUR)

A Walk in

El Rio Abajo Rio [1]

I GOT PREGNANT READING Dr. Clarissa Pinkola Estés's book.

No, I'm not claiming virgin birth. My son, Jean-Paul, is mortal and my husband, David, was very much involved. And, yes, I realize this is a book about menopause, not about pregnancy. But I warned you in the very beginning that it was also a book about change and transformation, and about a woman's ability to create.

Even though our culture does not currently recognize it, when a woman taps into her inner soul, into her fundamental spirit, she connects to a massive and credible power. Simply put, when this power is unleashed, strange, wonderful, and unexpected things can and will happen.

This is what I mean when I write that I got pregnant reading Dr. Estés's book. It's true that I was already headed in that direction. I was already walking down that particular spiritual road. But Estés picked me up and gave me a ride. The words and stories in *Women Who Run with the Wolves*[2] helped liberate my soul from the grips of psychic isolation. They changed the way I thought and perceived and the manner in which I responded to the universe, and so allowed into my life that which had never been before.

---

[1] "*El Rio Abajo Rio,* the river beneath the river," from the poem "Rowing Songs for The Night-Sea Journey," © 1970, Clarissa Pinkola Estés, Prairie Forever Press.
[2] Estés, Clarissa Pinkola. *Women Who Run with the Wolves,* Ballantine Books, New York, 1992.

It all began years ago.

In addition to being a lyrical writer and champion of the feminine spirit, Dr. Estés is an award-winning poet, a *cantadora*, an internationally recognized scholar, and a senior Jungian psychoanalyst. When I first met her she was the executive director of the C. G. Jung Center for Education and Research in the Rocky Mountains, and had taught and been in clinical practice for over two decades. She had begun writing *Women Who Run with the Wolves* in 1971. The manuscript, which took over twenty years to complete, contains twenty of her unique, dark, and erotic tales along with her lyric psychoanalytic commentaries.[3] But prior to its publication in 1992, challenged by rejection after rejection from publishers, she had recorded and released small portions of this work on audiocassettes by the same title.[4] At the time, I was publisher of a regional psychology magazine in Colorado. On a chilly February day in 1990, I interviewed Estés for an article on education. Afterward, I took home a set of her tapes for review in the magazine. Curious and intrigued, I listened to the cassettes before sending them off to the reviewer. Then I promptly went out and bought my own set.

The years went by, but I never forgot those tapes. Or Estés. When I found myself in California, happily married but sadly childless, forty-three and experiencing my first menopausal symptoms, I felt deep despair at the ending of my fertility. I took the audiocassettes off my shelf and listened to them. I was certain that somewhere in her words, imbedded in images or woven into text, was the salve to soothe my menopausal sorrow.

My objective was to come to terms with my existence as it was, no matter what pains, what sorrows, what fears. I wanted to take the

[3] It was part of a massive manuscript of 100 tales on the inner life that ran to 2,200 pages.

[4] Estés, Clarissa Pinkola. *Women Who Run with the Wolves* (Audio), Sounds True Recordings, Boulder, Colorado, 1989.

journey life was offering me, to stop resisting everything, and to accept the conditions staring me in the face. I wanted to travel *into* my life not away from it, so I could find the inherent gifts and truth of my existence. But I was struggling with both fear and grief.

The stories Estés created on those audios, in what some call "one of the greatest healing voices of our time," were powerful. For me, they acted like tiny pinpoints of light on a cold, dark night. They were small but potent beacons that awakened memories containing the directions home. As I listened, I was soon filled with renewed hope—not that I would become pregnant, but that I was going to make it, make it through what seemed to be my fate, and make it through the menopausal passage intact and able to live a joyful life again.

Somewhere during the process of listening to her tapes and reading her book, my life changed. A wish was fulfilled and I became pregnant with David's child. You can laugh it off as coincidence if you want, or tell me I'm drawing a connection where none exists, but I believe there's more truth to my words than not. Admittedly, I'm not the first menopausal woman to have a baby and I won't be the last. It's not a scientific miracle. But it is, for me, miraculous. Why, at the age of forty-three, after years of making love without contraceptives, after having my menstrual periods stop altogether and other menopausal symptoms begin, why would I suddenly become pregnant?

I think it's because if you let life happen, you'll find the universe is full of miracles. I think it's because we are actually more powerful than we dare dream. And I think it's because Estés taught me to sing.

In her audio works and in the very first chapter of *Women Who Run with the Wolves,* Estés tells her original tale of *La Loba,* the wolf woman, an old crone who roams the deserts gathering bones. When *La Loba* is ready, when her gathering is done, she sings over the bones of a wolf and brings it back to life. Flesh, fur, breath both moist and hot—the resurrected wolf leaps up and runs off out into the desert night and as it does, it turns into a beautiful, laughing woman.

Estés calls her *La Loba*, a *cuento milagro*, a miracle story, and explains how "'to sing' means to use one's soul voice. It means to say on the breath the truth of one's power and one's need."[5] Sitting in her cave, singing as she does, *La Loba* breathes life into the wolf's bones, she breathes spirit into its body, she breathes that which is the very essence of life. When this singing is done, the bones and the creature that once was, are transformed.

This is possible because *La Loba* is a mother of a different kind, giving life not through physical birth, but through spiritual birth. She's past her childbearing days but not past her life–bearing years.

I'd had glimpses of and encounters with such power before, but Estés was reaffirming it for me, naming it, giving it a form that I could grasp. The message was that we all possess the potential of *La Loba,* not just metaphorically, not just in our dreams, but in our everyday and ordinary life. Clearly, Estés's story of *La Loba* says that we can resurrect our souls, we can transform our inner lives, and we can bring forth our creations into the world.

As I continued listening to and reading her work, my awareness of what Estés calls in her poems "*El rio abajo rio*" ("the river beneath the river") began to swell. Being interested in matters of the spirit, I had known about this force for a long time although I referred to it as something else. Estés's perspective on it, however, allowed me to see it through more trusting eyes and to experience it in a new way. I understood her image, "*El rio abajo rio,*" as the life that creates life, the spiritual wind that blows the earthly gale into being. Although I could touch it, experience it, and be helped by it, it remained in the other world, that powerful place I could sometimes visit but in which I did not live.

[5] Estés, *Women Who Run with the Wolves,* page 28.

In her book, Dr. Estés explained that "*El rio abajo rio*" is the place (in the psyche) where visitations, miracles, imaginations, inspirations, and healings of all nature occur. I remember nodding my head in agreement. Yes, I understood. I'd been there. At various times, I'd been so healed and so inspired. But then Estés called the river *La Loba*'s home. Home? When she did that, when Estés used the word *home*, an old, old door in my own psyche creaked open.

And through that door walked *El duende*.

Estés defines *El duende*, a Spanish term similar to "muse," as the quixotic force behind a person's life-filled actions and creative life. It is a power very much greater than the self but which is inclusive of self at the same time. According to Estés, *El duende* is the magical force that whispers in our ears and feeds our souls so that we can create. It's another perspective on "*El rio abajo rio*," another way to gain the ability to bring forth what's inside. And I believe what Estés so aptly said to me upon hearing the news of Jean-Paul's impending arrival. She squinted at me, and with a slight cackle said, "*El duende* came into your life and filled your mind with a book, and your belly with a baby."

The images of *La Loba, El duende,* and "*El rio abajo rio*" contain the secrets of creative life and it is this magic of resurrection, this gift of creative birth, that is Estés's legacy. It is why I traveled back to the Rocky Mountains to talk with her and why *Red Moon Passage* would not be complete without her voice.

These ideas concerning creation are particularly pertinent to older women because as we make the menopausal passage, the wall between the physical realm and the spiritual realm grows thinner. It's not that younger women can't connect with such power, because clearly some do. And it's not that younger women shouldn't, because they should. But one of the gifts of midlife, of menopause, is that it can become easier to be touched by this force.

And so it was on a chilly November morning that I knocked on the door of Dr. Estés's home. The sky was overcast with gray and there was a sprinkling of snow on the ground. But not all the birds had flown south. A small jay watched me from a tree.

Estés opened the door and her warmth spilled out and embraced me. She's a large woman, and although she'd demur, she's a beautiful woman. If you've ever met her or simply watched her from afar as you listened to her speak or perform, you understand what I mean. Her beauty comes from deep within her soul and it surrounds her with a powerful aura that makes you want to step closer and never let her out of your sight.

It was so good to see her again and we laughed about my growing tummy. She laid her warm hands on my belly, paused for a moment looking skyward, and pronounced, "It's a good one. You will indeed have a fine child."

I told her it was her fault and we laughed again. But then I explained about the sadness I had experienced when I started into menopause, how I'd resigned myself to growing old and dying without ever having given birth. "I cried and cried," I said. "It was such a tremendous loss. But after listening to your tapes and reading your book, I worked hard to make peace with myself about it— not to give up and retreat like a wounded animal, but to fully accept my circumstances so I could move forward. And then, all of a sudden, here's this child."

"*El duende*," Estés declared. "*El duende*."

We went inside and made ourselves comfortable in her parlor, in overstuffed furniture before a small fire. There, we talked for many hours. Keep reading now and Estés will tell you in her own voice that if we will not back off and run away, if we will affirm our truths and keep the process going, then women experiencing menopause can knowingly and consciously walk in *El rio abajo rio*. We can dance with *El duende* and sing over any bones we choose.

Literally translated *El duende* means "the goblin wind" behind all creative life. It is the spirit, the immense spirit, often understood as a force of all that is, all that can be, all that will ever be. In another tongue it might be called *espiritu sanctu*, "the Holy Ghost"; in yet another language it might be called the *Piscis sophia*, or *Ruach*, "the breath of God," or the *Hagia sophia*, "the wind of knowing."

It is said that *El duende* can split a person's heart and mind wide open, that it can descend to inspire a person, to shake or impregnate a person, or to put something into a person that they have been emptied of or that they have never had before, like grace for instance. *El duende* is both the restorer and the new action. *El duende* is the passion and the quickening. *El duende* is the ashes stirring again. *El duende* is the lover and the lovemaking and the life born from the lovemaking. It is everything.

How does it choose whom to descend upon? Aye, it comes to the one who has laid out food for it, the one who has left the door open for it, the one who yearns for such a guest. You can beckon *El duende* into your life by walking many different pathways. The road of the artist, the road of the priest, the road of the poet, the road of the lover of beauty, the road of the lover of the life force and of God.

The spiritual *padrino* ("godfather") of my life is a poet, Federico Garcia Lorca. He once traveled from Spain to Cuba in order to teach. In Havana, he gave a lecture on *El duende*.[6] Some did not understand what he was trying to say. Some thought he was being fatuous. It was popular at that time among the literati to call images

---

[6]I give thanks to Dr. Stella Rodruiquez for her translation, "from The Havana Lectures, 1928."

of God and the forces of God—from which the concept of *El duende* derives—foolish, to protest that ideas such as these were useless unless they could be used for political or financial purposes, unless they reflected ruling class ideals of beauty and power.

El duende, however, is an earthy idea, one that lives from its roots upward; though it may have been conceived in heaven, it is rooted deep in the earthy quality of human beings.

"Ah," said Lorca by way of bringing his listeners down to earth, down into the fertile mud where the forces of *El duende* thrive, "*Duende* can even overcome inexperience and poor material. There was once a flamenco contest. . . . In this *concurso de baile* ["dance contest"] at Jerez, the bouts were won by an eighty-year-old woman, even though she was competing against beautiful young women *con las cinturas de agua,* with waists like flowing water. The old one simply stepped forward, raised her arms, threw her head back, and stamped the floor of the stage."

In this way, *with what was inside her,* rather than *with what was on the outside of her,* the old woman was gladly given the crown. The old one was filled to the spilling point with *El duende.*

From my point of view, a person gives their life to the cultivating of the spirit, *El duende.* We do not have far to travel, it is born into each person—some are born with a seed of it, others with a raging sea of it.

It has also been said by some of the old people in our family that when you die, if you wish to be part of *El duende,* you can. One would choose by an act of intention while living, to be part of *El duende* in the time after life. Then, one would spend their incorporeal life, their life without a body, being a part of the wind that moves people who are embodied . . . one would become a part of the force that inspires human beings.

I tell you lightheartedly, but also seriously, if there is a possibility after this life, I think this is something I would like to do—

hover over the poet who is struggling, over the one who is inventing, over the one who is praying for a vision of how it all goes together. And suddenly, since we disembodied inspiratrices live in "the land of Aha," we send down on a breeze or in a firestorm, the idea, the solution, the missing piece, and there! the person is filled, or taken away out of the ordinary, or shaken up just right.

Imagine Bonnie writing at her desk. She is pausing or reflecting, and maybe even struggling a little bit. So then the inspiratrice would float around her and suddenly infuse her—vooom! And she would say, "Ah yes," and write furiously. Then one would have done one's work as a part of *El duende*.

Some days and nights I have wanted to see the face of the one who has come to me so that the words and the work that come out of my pen continue to flow. It is not me alone. It is certainly not I, and it is not only I. Who has come? Who continues to come? No one has ideas enough or breath enough or depth enough to do all of creative life by themselves. My visitor, *mi invitada*, is *mi duende*, my Invited One.

BLOOD AND ROSES

At this point, Estés and I laughed as we speculated on who else (with the help of El duende, *of course) could have written* Women Who Run with the Wolves. *Muse or no, I don't believe anyone else could have written it. Dr. Estés's journey through life and the choices she made—all the particular pains, sorrows, and joys she's dealt with and how she dealt with them—culminated in the unique and powerful understanding of life she now possesses. It's why I chose her for this book.*

In addition to this knowledge and understanding of the workings of the universe, there is a second reason that makes her most qualified to speak on the subject of the Red Moon Passage. Estés went through menopause very early and very painfully. But unlike some, she reached the other side of this journey intact, aware and blossoming with incredibly increased abilities. I asked her to talk about that experience, the time she calls sangre y rosas, *"the time of blood and roses."*

I hesitate to tell of this time in a public manner, in part for being a deeply private person, knowing that people will read this, and feeling it is one of the great mysteries of my world and of my life. The only thing that makes me reveal some of what I ordinarily would not share with one, let alone tell to many, is that I would never want another young woman to be without firsthand advice on this particular kind of dark night.

Though dreams alone can be sturdy guides, it is a mercy of the deepest kind to have at your side one who knows, one who has gone before on the road, instead of one who guesses, one who surmises and does not really know.

Though I cannot tell you all things, not all the night dreams, nor all the day visitations, for some of these are working mysteries to me yet and they must remain so, let us see what I can tell you that might be of pragmatic use to another who entered, as I did, a dark night unexpectedly.

At age thirty-three, partly as a result of the fatally flawed medical climate concerning the safety of intrauterine devices, I came to a life-threatening illness. After multiple misdiagnoses over a year's time of hemorrhaging, I was again misdiagnosed as having incomplete miscarriages. I submitted to D&C.

Regardless, I continued to hemorrhage, had raging fevers, but somehow continued to work, raise my family, and go to school, studying very hard and long. I was determined to complete my education. But, I felt very, very poorly. The marrow of my bones burned like fire, I was breathless. I felt as though I had a devastating flu day after day after day. My vision was narrowing. I had immense night sweats and unrelieved headaches. I was far from home, far from the insights and help of my grandmothers and aunts.

One morning as I rose from my bed, I sank to the floor and could not go on. My mind was clear, but my body was broken completely. I could not move.

I had become so weak from loss of blood that if a fire had broken out I would not have been able to flee. If the roof had collapsed, I would not have been able to save myself nor anyone else.

In the emergency room, a doctor diagnosed life-threatening anemia. My hematocrit was less than half of what it ought to be. The IUD had perforated my uterus, and my reproductive organs were badly damaged and other viscera as well. The gravest difficulty was peritonitis, and it was this that finally brought my body crashing down. From that moment, and for a long time afterward, I danced with death in various sambas, rumbas, and free-style ways.

Before surgery, I was a thirty-three-year-old woman who loved children and wanted to have more. After surgery, I was catapulted into instant menopause, my childbearing years stripped away in a few hours' time, literally cut away, my life given back to me, yes, but as one would come across a shred of rag and a scrap of bone thrown down in a heap. It was death that had overtaken me.

But as I would learn, it was that journey with dry-boned death that brought me to understandings that are rare and unusual, that ultimately brought me back to life, and into a new life, the old life and the old ignorances gone forever.

The surgery I'd had was more literally a hysterectomy, salpingectomy, and an oophorectomy, which is the removal of the ovaries. I was shocked when I read my medical report because it called the surgery "female castration."

When ovaries are removed, not the uterus so much, although I think there is a change in women when their uteri are removed too, but it is the removal of the ovaries that causes menopause. Instant menopause.

It was a remarkable experience to be so very ill, so hurting and in lightning-bolt pain, and then to awaken after surgery and have a different kind of pain altogether. And ten additional kinds of deep psychic pain. I did not expect them to remove my ovaries and fallopian tubes, just the uterus and part of the bowel because of the scarring caused by the missile IUD.

To awaken and be told, "Well, we had to take everything, your entire reproductive system"—this was deeply shocking.

Before the surgery I had had an argument with the surgeon. He said, "We're going to do a T-incision on you. That means we are going to cut you from the sternum down to the pubic bone and then from hip to hip because you're a fat woman and we can't take any chances and I wish you weighed less because it's a very dangerous surgery." And on and on he ranted.

I was very young, and I grew up in the so-called "underclass," the working class, where we were taught to unequivocally obey anyone who had more education and authority than we. But something in me said this was a moment when all old rules must be shattered.

I pulled myself up on one elbow and croaked in a whisper that made my head feel like it would blow apart, "You are not going to do that. You are going to do the regular incision that goes lateral from hip to hip and if I wake up with a T-incision . . . I will sue you from here to . . . [I was going to say Constantinople, but I did not have enough breath left in my body for all those syllables] . . . New . . . York."

This definitely snagged his attention. Not the suing part (actually I hadn't the faintest idea about how to go about suing anything more than the hogs back home). The surgeon was furious. His face turned purple, and then magenta, and then claret red. His veins stuck out like big blue snakes all over his head and neck. His words and his high-dungeon tone of voice are burned into my brain. He screeched, "You will not dictate to me on matters of medical importance."

But I managed somehow to whisper back, "Then I will choose

to die because I will not have this surgery. My blood is on your hands."

So that's the way it began, by my taking a stand. I knew that to cut through all those layers of muscle, tissue, and body fat would cause the wound to take an extra long time to heal. A long, long time. I had a friend who had had a T-incision. She was a big woman like myself and one side of her stomach and abdomen healed slightly higher than the other. Now she has a "step" that goes across her upper abdomen (the surgery was on her lower abdomen), an unnecessarily long and grotesque scar. I have seen many women with scars placed in ways that a careful and thoughtful surgeon would not have placed them. There is no reason for surgeons not to learn to operate on all kinds of body configurations, on all ages of people, on all ethnic groups with all their differences in body type and scar formation and so forth.

I argued with the doctor as a deep response to his disrespect of the female body, of my female body. I was frightened at the words that came out of my mouth. I knew within hours I was going to allow this man to hold my life in his hands. I feared him. But more, I feared his continuing to, in my opinion, recklessly carve up other men and women with no respect or attention to their spirits, souls, and bodies—all of a piece—my spirit, soul, and body included.

(I know from previous conversations that Estés had other arguments with the doctor. She insisted the hospital give her her own organs they removed from her body. Later, she gently buried them in the ground as part of a healing ceremony. In the late 1970s such actions were rare, but Estés lets "El rio abajo rio" guide her and she fights to follow her instincts, no matter what other people say.)

The anesthesiologist was an old man who looked for all the world like the proverbial village doctor—white hair, bushy eyebrows, kind eyes. He asked, "How much do you weigh?" and bent down so I could tell him. As he prepared all the various tubes, he talked about his prized horse, a mare that he loved and who was so gentle. I remember falling into that throat-burning sleep of fumes whispering, "Please treat me as if I were your fine Tennessee walking horse."

There are many parts to this time of my life, but I think one aspect that would be germane to others is that when I awoke from this surgery, I'd never been in so much pain in my entire life. Pain like a firestorm in all the most tender flesh, pain like being thrown up in the air and falling down on sharpened pikes, pain like being cut deep, without anesthesia. I made up a million metaphors in my mind in order to attempt to define the pain and thereby release myself from it. The physician knew that I was massively sensitive to painkilling medication, that there were certain painkillers—Percodan, Darvon—that I could not take without extremities going numb, without all the symptoms of poisoning. But he insisted on giving them to me anyway and in large doses. I felt deeply and psychically invaded with images and feelings that were massively disturbing. These many years later I now understand that I was being overdosed, poisoned actually, and was alternately "having the mental bends" and "crashing" off the drugs.

The drugs caused a psychic disorganization that was so profoundly painful that I was beside myself. Although the media portrayed persons of my generation as "children of the Sixties," I had never taken hallucinatory drugs, it wasn't in my lifestyle hopes and dreams, nor among my values, so I had no idea. If I had been experienced in the drug culture, perhaps I would have known I was crashing and that the crashing was causing tremendous psychic pain. The psychic pain was so great that I could not imagine why I should go on living one more minute. It was very difficult to bear. It is even more difficult to explain to anyone who has not experienced it.

Finally after several long, hard days of feeling half-drowned and half-burned to the ground, I figured it out, and when the nurse delivered the big pill in the little white pleated cup, I hid it in the pillowcase. I tried to blend with the pain of my body rather than sustain the pain of a synthetic distortion of psyche. I prayed. Prayer helped immensely. I asked for visitors. Visitors came, kept coming, around the clock.

My dreams during this time, both leading up to and during this watershed event were dazzling, startlingly brilliant, and rich. I felt that my dream life was supporting me and helping me to realize what was going on. One of the dreams I had was about a young boy who came with a white bandage all around his head and an armful of roses, like *La Señora Teresa de las rosas*. The young boy said to me, "Look." He unwrapped his bandage and underneath he was whole; his injury was healed.

This is how I came to understand that I could bear this event, this cutting away of my young life resource in a way that was clearly irretrievable. This mystical and concentrated image, and others, made it more possible to realize that I could somehow bear the unbearable, and that I could be whole and clear without this brain-boggling medication, that there was a perfectly whole body underneath it all.

There were other events significant to me, some merely comedic, some startling, others profound.

For instance, during this time, my heart fibrillated and for a few moments I was gone. This is a three-volume story in itself.

At another time, my hospital roommate began to die during the night. Orthodox priests all dressed in black arrived past midnight in their tall hats and long beards, and their love and kindnesses to her blessed me as much as they blessed my poor roommate.

She died, not with the usual death rattle, but with just an incredibly long sigh. I had heard this long sigh before as many of our own old ones had died at home. Now I was in the anteroom of both life and death myself.

Another time a technician accidentally lacerated and spilled an entire bag of blood all over me as I was in the midst of my fifth transfusion. I had transfusions from late 1979 through 1980. These many years later, people speak of blood donor contamination back then. The only thing I have ever felt is grateful for those who donated their blood to me. Every now and then when I am extremely tired and do not bounce right back, I wonder, but then no, I think—the boychild with the armful of red roses was whole.

It was a long hospitalization. Every chance I could, I made my staggering way, in my funny hospital gown with tiny blue hexagons all over it, down to the chapel. The nurses teasingly began calling me "Night Walker." If there was a figure in white limping down the dark hall in the middle of the night, it was probably that young woman, the oophorectomy, hysterectomy, salpingectomy from 333 on her way to talk to her God. In the chapel, how could my Blessed Mother even understand me in my drugged state? I wondered. I thanked *mi Guadalupe* over and over for my life—for giving me life, for returning it to me again. *Oh mi Mami, muchisimas gracias. Please heal me and all others like me. . . .*

DESCENT TO THE UNDERWORLD

In terms of menopause, when finally this period of extreme pain (physical) passed, I could concentrate on the rather remarkable phenomenon of instant night sweats, instant hot flashes. Also, then came finally a profound depression. I was not receiving estrogen, and I must say that when, forty-eight hours after surgery, my body had depleted its estrogen, I could feel things I had never felt before—physically and mentally.

I know this is a curious way of telling this. It was a dark, dark time, a terrifying time, yet with a great unwavering light at the center of it all. One of the things that was most remarkable was that the thinness of the membrane between my unconscious and conscious mind reminded me of how I used to feel premenstrually. A few days before one's period starts, many women, including myself, had an extreme sensitivity and a pressure to make an evaluation of one's life as it is now and what one wished it had been, and what has gone well and what has not gone well, and what one hoped for the future.

I don't like PMS as a descriptive term for every nonordinary feeling and thought that comes along during such a time. I don't care much for those who feel determined to pathologize what I think is often and actually, in metaphoric terms, a descent to the underworld, an opportunity for mystical experience. While it is true that there are pathologies associated with some women's premenstrual tension, and that that is real and bedeviling and very difficult to the person who suffers from it, more so, this is a period of time every few weeks that is generous in its capacity for deep feeling, for valuation and reevaluation of one's works and intentions.

But instead of descending into this kind of self-examination for two or three days at a time—which is a natural endeavor—this sensation of a kind of "premenstrual sensitivity" stretched over an entire year. It was penetrating. It was in certain ways daunting. And gravid with meanings. There was no happiness in it. There could not be because, for all practical purposes, I was dead, hanging on the world tree[7] just as assuredly as any mortal of the tales of old suffered and died to the world and awakened in another. My life as I had known it was over. I did not know if there would be another. Of course I would dance and sing and make love again, and joy-

---

[7] According to Funk and Wagnall's *Standard Dictionary of Folklore, Mythology and Legend,* Yggdrasil (from Scandinavian mythology) is the sacred ash tree that overshadows the entire universe; its roots and branches bind heaven and hell, earth, and the nether-regions, together. The roots of Yggdrasil lie in Hel; the trunk ascends through the Midgard—the earth. Rising through the mountain known as Asgard, it branches into the sky—its leaves are the clouds in the sky and its fruits are the stars.

fully. I was fully aware of that. These are not the kinds of questions I was asking. I was asking *mi Guadalupe, "Enséñame? por favor?"*— Show me? Please show the path, even just the next step. I understood this menopause as far more than a physical change—change, "the change," it is a misnomer. It is a descent and an arising. It is a sunset. Then, a sunrise. The time in between the two counts for everything.

I knew so many myths and folk tales and family tales about women in their descent being killed and hanging their skin on a spike in the underworld, that I had some skinny sense of where I was going. I was listening to my dreams and they were constantly showing various images of people who were well, people who were whole even though they appeared to have endured some kind of great suffering or sudden injury.

In one dream there was a dog, a wonderful large dog, limping, looking quite pathetic, and as it passed me by, it winked. I understood this dream this way: it hurts, it is painful, it is real, but there is an inner core, too, one that is strong, valuable, and to some extent quixotic and even funny.

I began taking estrogen about six months after the surgeries. It took a long time to adjust the doses properly, in part because my body and mind are extremely sensitive to drugs. And I had a hard time convincing the doctors to pay attention, to try to understand that we should start with small amounts and work our way up.

The doctors, however, did not start little. They gave Estés estrogen in large doses, and the result was a disaster. Speaking in a high, loud voice, throwing her arms about and wearing an exaggerated smile on her face, Estés made believe she was a crazed teenager from Southern California. We both laughed. She told me how the experience reminded her of a fairy tale she was given by a beloved old woman at a fishing camp where people fished in both summer and winter. Then, Estés told the tale.

There was a blind boy whose old grandmother was trying to kill him. She didn't want to hunt for him and he couldn't hunt for himself, so she was starving him to death. The grandmother went out every day and killed something to eat, but she told the boy that she didn't find anything.

One day a loon came to the boy's bedroom and told this story. "Long ago your father had set a snare and when I was trapped in it, I said to your father, 'I have children.' Your father said, 'Oh, well, that's all right then, I will not kill you. Go to your children.' And so I flew away. I know that your father has died and your mother also, and that you have been left with this grandmother."

The loon knew the boy was weak and starving to death. She said, "I'm going to take you to the lake, so get on my back."

The boy and the loon flew to a black, icy lake. The loon said, "Now hold on," and she dove down into the lake. Way down. The boy thought his lungs were going to burst and that he was going to die, but then suddenly she surfaced and flew high into the air and said, "Tell me, boy, what do you see?"

He looked around and he said, "I see shadows and a little bit of light."

The loon said, "Oh, that is not enough. We have to do it again." So she dove down under the lake with him again, and again he felt like his lungs might burst and that he would die. She surfaced finally at the last second and said, "Now tell me, boy, what do you see?"

He looked and said, "I see the hairs on the hills miles away. I believe there are 732 of them. And I see the flies in the air that are over my dead uncle's house."

And the loon said, "Oh, no, that's too much. We have to do it again." So she dove under the lake with the boy on her back and came up at the last second again, just when he thought he was going to die. She said, "What do you see now?"

And he said, "Well, I think if I look very hard I can imagine the flies around my dead uncle's house and I think if I put my mind to it I could count many of the grasses on the hill across the way."

The loon said, "That's perfect," and took him home.

The boy pretended that he was still blind and his grandmother said, "Come, bring your father's bow and arrow. There are three bears outside." When the boy brought them, she said, "All right, now aim from the left of your body." He did and she said, "Oh, you missed." But really, the bear went down. Then she said, "All right, now aim from the middle of your body. Quickly." He let the arrow fly and the middle bear was killed. But she said, "Oh, you missed again." And it was the same with the one on the right. "Oh, you missed."

But the boy, since his sight had been restored, saw that the bears were obviously dead. So he turned to his grandmother and said, "My sight has been restored and you are a wicked woman."

She begged for his forgiveness. He was a truly kind person, you see, and forgave her. Then he went hunting for the rest of their lives together. He provided the food and took care of her.

The grandmother went through the torture of a person who has another person be kind to them after they have tried to do them harm, and so was redeemed. And the boy went through life with this vision that is beyond the usual. And he knew the happiness of great generosity of heart.

This is somewhat how it felt to me. It felt like my "crossing over" in so many ways gave me insights, a vision, a gift of envisioning that I had never had as deeply before. I realized that I and others in our culture were being methodically starved of substance, that something was awry in some of the "wisdom" of our culture, that it did not have our best interests at heart, that it saw those who are "menopausal" as somehow less. It is not so, we are instead *more*. Much, much more.

I felt that if one could stand the suffering and the pain, if one could stand and understand the misunderstandings between culture and spirit, then visionary ability could be ours to keep. But, as in the story, it may take feeling that one has practically died at least three times.

A NEW DESTINY

Pregnancy. No more. Never to be pregnant again. Never a child again to be born through my body. This was great sorrow to me. There are many mothers with whom I share a common experience, that is, the entire time of being pregnant we feel we have met our destiny as humans ensouled in flesh, that this supreme and divine miracle of pregnancy allows us the greatest closeness known between God and humans, that is, being the flesh to soul co-creator of life.

I felt a thousand regrets, a thousand sorrows. Each one needing mending and time. Much, much time. We speak of childbearing loss. Why do we never speak of life-bearing loss?

The physicians prescribed estrogen to me because of my youth, and their fear that in one so young, age thirty-three, osteoporosis would result. Despite the estrogen, my body began to change dramatically. Within a year after surgery my skin had aged dramatically. I could hardly look at my hands and believe they were mine. My hair became very thin and I experienced what I felt were deep bone changes. I felt joint aches and hurt, and these continue to this day, almost twenty years later. I don't know how to explain it, but I thickened somehow in my joints. I experienced various things mentally that I always identified with being much older rather than the age that I was. I had become a young old woman.

But I must say, my spirit became far more fluent, multilingual, and I felt free to ask burning questions. There was a tremendous acceleration in my consciousness, so fast that I felt as though I had to hold on, that my hair and clothes were flying behind me as though I stood in a great wind—a wind of enormous change. I have a series of many drawings that I created during that time. They are of all things dying, all things folding and unfolding, the tiniest growing tall, the largest receding into the horizon line, and around the edges of many, a brilliant crimson or bright green circle.

There were many events that could be considered watershed in some way. A few I can say here. One was the realization that aging was accelerated. It was like time-lapse photography. I watched the skin of my eyes become crepey within a couple months. My fingernails changed. They became ridged and thicker. My lips lost some of the fat in the upper lip and I bruised much more easily. I think these dramatic changes in appearance accelerated my consciousness. It was as though becoming thinner in the skin, the hair, the bones,— somehow lets the soul shine through more. Also, the rapid change with yet a youthful spirit caused me to understand entirely and first-hand how the body may age, but the spirit is young forever.

The grief of knowing I would never bring another child from my body, that hot, steaming child, that new soul brought into the world, this knowledge, too, seemed to accelerate matters of psyche and insight. What different kinds of new life, what other kinds of great work might now be born of this body and spirit? What destiny would I serve now? I felt certain that God did not bring humans into being in order to live lives of quiet or frenzied desperation forever. For a time, yes. Even for a long time. But not forever.

It was required that I stay underground, and I did so for the better part of a decade. I moved from a sunny office to a north-facing one. There the air was darker, but clearer. I came to love this bluish light, the way we artists love the north-facing windows for showing us the colors of our palette true.

I needed immense amounts of introverted time. I was in a six-year-long psychoanalytic training program at that time at a training institute in the United States. It was a little excruciating because many of the training analysts knew what I had experienced and each one wanted to interpret my experiences with life and death—

each in their own manner—until I was nearly driven mad by all the conflicting ideas aimed at me.

They were trying to be helpful. But this was a journey meant for one, and in solitude. I dove deeper, swam far, far, faaaaaar out, and by fleeing those too easy and wildly speculative interpretations and intrusions, found my true home.

It was in this far encampment, far from others (except my closest family members), yet *baptizein,* buried, baptized in the pragmatic day-to-day living of a life and observing every nuance—this is where I still live, at the challenging edge of the village, not in the easy midst. I prefer it immensely. Here the water is cold and clear and to my liking.

I still take a minuscule, almost placebo, amount of estrogen—a tiny colored pill, which is the smallest dose made. I take half of this. I forget it sometimes for four, five, or ten days in a row. However, if I stop entirely at this point in my life, I can feel a bad change in my bones. I remain vigilant to what feels adequate and what does not.

In the end, all of what I experienced in "my old age while young," was "sitting in the fire without anesthesia."[8] Accelerated consciousness. Opportunity of vision. Coming through a fire awake instead of drugged or asleep. Something comes from hanging upside down in the underworld. Something great is born to those cut away so early. If you will die long enough, deep enough, some great sea change takes place—bringing bounty. Forever. I do not know if we can choose this path. More so, I would say certain ones are chosen.

The way that I understand the physiological, psychological, and spiritual aspects of menopause is that there are many layers to the process and that some women will experience one layer, and some will experience none and others yet will experience all layers. I

[8] From the poem "At the Asylum" © 1970, C. P. Estés.

think a great deal of what and how a woman experiences this time of life has something to do with one's constitution emotionally and spiritually to begin with. Women who experience all the layers—for instance, the emotional layer of loss of reproductive function, the physical layer of change in beauty, not loss of beauty, but change in beauty, and the layer of what I call in one of my poems "crossing the crone line"[9] of consciousness, crossing the psychic line—these can leave lasting and deep impressions. I'm certain they constitute doorways to one's new life.

THE HANDLESS MAIDEN

One of the ideas in Women Who Run with the Wolves *that truly intrigued me was Estés's chart of feminine states of consciousness. She assigns the chronological age of forty-two to forty-nine to the period of "early crone/finding the far encampment/giving courage to others." In the second half of her list are such states of consciousness as "becoming the watchwoman," the age of the "underworld, understanding the weaving of life," and the age of "less to saying, more to being." These phrases evoked the image of the old woman that I had seen that night in Colorado and seemed to describe her in ways for which I had not found words.*

Estés wrote that, "For many women, the first half of these stages of a woman's knowing, say to about forty or so, clearly moves from the substantive body of instinctual infant realizations to the bodily knowing of the deep mother. But in the second round of phases, the body becomes an internal sensing device almost exclusively and women become more and more subtle."[10]

Because these stages can help us name menopause more accurately, I asked Estés if she would please say more.

---

[9]From poem "Who Will Be at the Crossroad?" © 1981, C. P. Estés.
[10] Estés, *Women Who Run with the Wolves,* pages 447–449.

I know that all we humans have a predilection to be told the five, or seven, or twenty stages of this or that, to discover the "real" secrets of life. The truth is that each person is a true custom endeavor. I do not think there is a five easy steps to anything. I do not believe we are in a maze for which we must find a solution, but rather in a story, a divine one, of, in, and through which we are to live to the fullest given to us.

Yet I do see, from the anecdotal evidence gathered from having lived with a dozen old women while I was growing up, from having had many psychoanalytic clients over the years who were far older than I, and from my own perceptions of these matters, that there are definite times of change of consciousness, change of awareness, deepening, shifting, remembering, reclaiming, sharpening, letting go, taking on, being. Being. Just being.

These states, stages, or changes are not tied to chronological age although they could be for many, but not for all. They represent, more, archetypal patterns that lead to maturity. They are patterns of mastery one might say, but they do not always assert themselves in women in nice neat rows because destiny plays a big part in what we might do next, what fantastic or limpid thing might be dropped into our lives.

As a general set of tools for understanding where one resides in the story of one's own life, certainly night dreams are essential. Expressive therapy, that is, the therapy of original art, is an expression of self. It is like a conversation with *La otra,* "the other." It is like having a friend who knows far more than you.

One needs also to have some way of expressing what is inside one and allowing it to rise on its own. Not trying to make something, but letting the drawing draw itself, letting the poem "poem" itself, letting your novel "novelize," that is, to "make new" itself, and see what it is then.

In one of my poems called "Commenting Before the Poems," there is a line, "Do not try so hard to think. / You are not writing a poem / Try hard instead 'to open'/ for the poem that is writing it-self through you."[11]

As tools for transformation, certainly these—dreams and expres-sive arts—are essential. And that descent to the underworld, that is, taking the journey to make conscious that which is unconscious. Taking the journey? Giving oneself time to think about one's life, what one has done, not done, where one is going, has not gone, what one wishes for, longs for, what one fears. And are the answers to these questions of enough weight to chart the course differently, just a little, or turn the ship around entirely? If one is uncomfortable with the word *underworld,* one can call it *examination,* one can call it *in-ventory,* one can call it *looking into oneself,* one can call it *appraisal,* one can call it *self-contemplation,* one can call it "*taking stock.*"

For women who are ready to make a descent, who are in tran-sition or in turmoil, there is a fairy tale I have reconstructed in my work *Women Who Run with the Wolves.* The tale is called "The Handless Maiden." Contained in it, in the version we tell in our family, is one of the best teaching medicines I know.

This story is about a woman whose father is tricked into mak-ing a pact with the devil. Father is to be rewarded with riches in exchange for the daughter's life. But in the end, he cannot give his child up and the unhappy compromise is that he is forced to cut off her hands. Rejecting her father's offer to protect her for the rest of her life and accepting her armless fate, the Handless Maiden sets out on the road. As she wanders the world, she is given many gifts. Trees bend to feed her, people clothe and shelter her. She ends up marrying a king who gives her a pair of silver hands. But the tale doesn't end there. While the king is away at war, she gives birth to a child. The king's mother sends a messenger to the battlefield to tell the king the good news, but the devil reappears and fouls the message so that the king, believing his wife to have sunken to a

---

[11] Excerpt from "Commenting Before the Poems" © 1970, C. P. Estés.

heinous level, sends back a message to the castle commanding that both queen and child are to be slain. The young queen flees with her child. She spends seven years in the forest, during which time her real hands, out of valiant courage, grow back. When the king returns from war, he finds out about the devil's plot. Overcome with grief, he goes off in search of his queen, suffering much but eventually finding her and their child alive and well in the forest. Finally, after so much travail, the family is reunited.

The psychic metaphors of this tale are strong and they speak clearly to what happens when we lose our way and how we can travel into the underworld, into the unconscious "forest realms," so to speak, to refind and regrow ourselves.

I think the underlying theme of this story as it is told in amplified episodes in *Women Who Run with the Wolves* is especially poignant for the menopausal period because it details every step of the way to great and long transitions and sudden changes.

The story is very long, and in our family it was told over many months' time, a little at a time. The amount of time that the Handless Maiden spends in the underworld is very long as well. She has specific tasks to fulfill that one can understand as the tasks of great spiritual transition and transformation. She suffers, she is insightful, she endures, she finds a way. It often takes us a long time after we lose our grasp of things, lose our hands, so to speak. It takes time and time and time to grow one's hands back again. I use this story in my healing work to talk about the ability to grasp what is happening to the individual in spite of the fact that their hands are missing, that they have lost touch or are out of reach or have lost their take on the world. The story details how when an entropy, a decline appears, ravages even, that other abilities, other dynamisms come to the fore. Sudden grace appears, sudden help comes from those invisible hands that lift us across the water that is too wide, too deep, and too cold for us to cross by ourselves. To have all these miraculous forces begin to gather, to feed you, nourish you, guide you, tell you, teach you—this is the mark of being in the descent, an authentic one, not a nice highly aesthetic exciting one, but a dry-boned, simple, humble one wherein one spends not a week-end, not a few weeks even, but day in and day out the time required to disassemble and reassemble oneself in the underworld, that is, the world that is not mundane, that is not of secular matters only.

The descent of a person's consciousness in order to shed the old and create a new consciousness is often canalized through dreams. The expressive life—your dance, your art, your sculpture, your writing, your whatever way you use to express yourself—is often canalized here as well. Imagine the creative life moving from the biological imperative of reproduction, menstruation, and so on to a psychic creative function that also has its times of filling and emptying, its times of conception, pregnancy, quickening, and birth. Understand that in menopause, there is no longer a physical form only. We are on spiritual ground where babies still arrive, but they are spiritual babies; blood still comes, but it is the river of all life; emptiness still comes, but it has moment and meaning, it is not just a vacancy at the interior hotel.

If we were all rulers of the world and magically had the eco-nomic, familial, and psychic wherewithal to do as we wished at the time of menopause, millions of women across the world would be-gin emigrating across the land, seeking a hospitable place to live out their menopause from a wider viewpoint; women would go away for a year, perhaps two. Good-bye dear husband, or annoying hus-band, good-bye grocery shopping on Tuesdays between 5 and 7 P.M. when traffic is lightest, good-bye the sludge of whatever drudgery I've sold myself into lock, stock, and barrel. Good-bye my dear children; wave at your mother as she "disappears into the stinging sun. . . ."[12]

Maybe the women would come back home from time to time

[12] From the poem "Stolen by Wolves" © 1980, C. P. Estés.

to touch base, to say hello, to make love, but for the most part, I think they would stay away so they could see without having all the static, all the drifting radio waves that go on when you are trying to do something and also have to work, sleep, and be with other people and your family and your house, and dust everything and work hard to insure what you dust, and to shine and polish things that may have meant something to you twenty or thirty years ago, but now are like hundreds of little yipping dogs demanding your attention.

Some women become upset to a degree when they enter menopause. I have seen women become cruel, or else beside themselves, with no one to tell them what they might do, what to expect, or what this time can be used for. With no one to guide or tell them, they are totally without help. This is not as it ought to be. The fact that such a vacuum exists is evidence of a great destruction from many directions to woman hand-me-down rites, rituals, and information about the stages of women's lives.

What are those who are isolated to do? I think that if they could listen to their dreams, that they would come through this deep-sea change with good direction. Over my years as a psychoanalyst, I've seen profound evidence that dreams give insights into our attitudes and processes. Also, whatever and whomever a woman has love for could help. Anything you are moved by, anything that you care for, through these, guidance can come.

GROWING OUR HANDS BACK

As in the tale, menopause is a time of having your hands cut off. Women have a way of relating to the world, of feeling and knowing with their bodies, and then suddenly it all begins to change. But can everyone grow their hands back? I asked Estés.

I think all women grow their hands back, but for some it is harder and longer. There is a mind-set that helps to grow the hands back.

And many aren't in any mind-set. They feel they are not even in their right mind.

I met a woman some time back. She was perhaps sixty-five years old, perhaps closer to seventy, and in most lights looked perhaps forty-five. She had had several face lifts. I think it is all right for women to have face lifts if they want to have them. But, it ought not be used to inhibit the certain psychic developments that come with age. As an artist, I could see a face lift as a kind of self-construction or self-decoration. But if it causes a stoppage or even a hemorrhage in consciousness, because one is pretending to be something one is not, it is hard to see how its benefits outweigh its potential drawbacks to realizing a new and strong life of soul and psyche.

The woman and I were talking. She had asked about my next book and I was telling her it was about the figure of the old woman in fairy tales. She was saying, "Well, this culture is so youth oriented . . . ," and off she went into a monologue that was both astonishing and heartrending for its bitterness.

"No," I said. "No, it isn't. I have never perceived our culture [my own ethnic culture] as youth oriented. I have perceived it far, far more as run by class than by youth." Our culture is oriented by and toward the ruling class, period. Class outstrips even race as the factor often used to distort what is just or decent or proper. All images held out as valuable or beautiful are mostly defined by the ruling class and whatever it has decided to value. There is a trickle-up effect only insofar as the overclass is fascinated with something the underclass must live with as a result of necessity, or something the poor have produced anew, or else held to be so for eons.

So we talked back and forth for a bit. Her question was, how can women—meaning, I think, herself—how can women have a real life in a culture that values only youth?

I said, only a small and visible part of our culture over-values youth. The rest values work, and spirit, and love. Which part of the culture will you choose? I suggested that one has to consider ceasing to value only one's youthful appearance, not stop valuing youthful appearance, but stop valuing *only* what is youthful, and begin valuing what is midway and far elder as well.

What she said in response made me feel very sad. She is married to a high-profile professional. He has had his friends lift and tuck her. She said, "I just can't just let myself go." And she meant, I can't let myself go, as in, let my hair hang in my face. But what I heard was that "I can't let go, I can't go on without this time-stopping subterfuge." And that was exactly where she was caught.

The problem is this: that of letting go of a fantasy that has never served women or men very well to begin with, and in fact, is not even quite true. That is the fantasy that only youth or youngness can generate love, heat, and solidarity between two persons or between a person and her or his public. It is hard to move on if you feel it is all you have, or that you can take nothing of it with you. And so the sad woman went on in a flood of words: "Well what do you mean? That I shouldn't 'take care' of myself? That I shouldn't care about how I look?"

What I heard were her husband's fears coming out of her mouth. Fears that she would not be arousing, and if she were not arousing, if his arousal centered on "the look of youth" only, then she would let him down—figuratively and literally perhaps—and that central barometer consulted by many, the hardness of the penis, would be diminished, and he would blame her. She would feel bad and he would feel bad, and if he were seeking to maintain "the hard-on of the universe," he might have to leave her to pursue "the one" who might momentarily fulfill his hope. So she ought to try very hard to help him by trying awfully hard to maintain "the look," rather than by learning to help him expand feeling to all parts of his body, to see and experience beauty in many ways, rather than only one way, to feel exquisite pleasure. If he is not able to expand his cues for arousal beyond *La papel,* "the paper women,"[13] then this is not her issue, but his. The sad woman, however, saw the entire matter as "a job, a chore" that accrued solely to her. She mistakenly thought the responsibility lay with her rather than with them both. In her maintaining "the appearance," and he giving the consequences of her doing this no deep thought, they had together robbed themselves utterly blind of the most lush and poignant years of life.

I have seen a couple things that initially were shocking, but I feel they were very important harbingers. I saw a stripper on television who was seventy years old. Did you see it? At first I had my hand over my mouth. I was saying: "*Mio dio, dio mio,* oh my God." All these emotions went through me. Suddenly I felt electrified. I was awed and appalled and happy and taken aback. Some of the women in the audience had wonderful looks on their faces and some had their hands over their eyes. And I thought, that is what needs to happen: the eroticism of all women and all men regardless of their ages.

(But not children. It is a despicable idea to eroticize young people for the pleasure of adults.)

Instead of saying that "she looks good for forty," "she looks good for fifty," or "she looks good for sixty," we need to move to an appreciation of many different forms of beauty—beauty that is beauty in its own class. Beauty that has its own features and dimensions, a broad spectrum rather than a narrow one, and especially one that is befitting to the millions, rather than to only one soul out of 6 million.

I have had a vision about what we need to see. What if the pas-

---

[13] *La papel* "the paper woman"—excerpt from poem "The Pornography Addict" © 1980, C. P. Estés.

sage through to new life started with something that most often seems outré to the woman's worldview? Go to college at age seventy? Sail the Inside Passage at my age? Buy that red dress? Begin over again? Allow myself to be truly alive? Stop being afraid to stand out? Or to turn inward? Whatever makes us jump back seems at the very least worthy of being examined carefully for its potential usefulness.

What if the debased way is to always stop at the point of the first "no, I couldn't do that, it's not for me"? What if instead we went ahead anyway, taking more chances in a time of life that we thought we'd run out of chances? What if we refused to believe we'd run out of chances? What if we went through the revulsion and repulsion, all that flailing around in some of one's long-held but no longer useful viewpoints, and came out into all the joyfulness that there is on the other side? I think resisting the living of the life impulse that urges us to remain alert, interested, creative, sexual, alluring, and confident for life—has in itself certainly contributed to all this disturbance we have about real age, that is, vibrant life. Maybe it is that we are constantly stopping the process, constantly stopping the process, constantly stopping the process. Initiation is not supposed to be easy. It is hard because it would not be initiation, that is, an education, if it were not. But it has to be a right kind, one that teaches the intrinsic value of the immense crossings in life. I certainly am not saying that acting as a stripper is the median pathway. But what about absolutely stripping away old attitudes and trying not to drag the feet so much but divesting oneself of uselessness with some sass. I am saying that, in whatever form, the body, too, has vibrant life as one makes this passage, has new and renewed life.

In certain ways, I have been an oldish woman since I was thirty-three years old. Almost two decades have passed since that time of death and dying and rebirth long ago. In menopause, I am certain we have the chance to merge with the greater self, that one, that reflective visionary one, who has been running along beside us all our lives long.

Estés says this and we look at each other, not saying a word, not moving, but both of us knowing that what she's just said is absolutely true. It's one of those moments of cognition when clarity emerges. I just lean back on the couch and breathe.

PART FIVE

We Are the Dream

and in the Dream

We Are Wise

I am alone, standing in an expanse of grassy plain. The grayish green world around me feels prehistoric; it is both now and a long time ago. A teepee sits in the grass some ways off and although the relationship is unclear, I recognize it as having something to do with me. Curious but also anxious, I start walking toward it.

As I get closer, my anxiety grows into fear but I am compelled forward by the familiarity. The teepee is made of white hide. Slowly, I pull open the flap and there is a tremendous roar. The earth trembles. Out of the teepee rushes a herd of bison. One after another after another they come—strong and powerful and wild. The huge black beasts gallop toward the horizon and then fly up to the stars.

I stand covered with their dust.

I experienced this vision in the summer of 1989. At the time, I was involved with a shamanic drumming group that met on Sunday evenings in a small church just a few blocks from my home. I took many journeys during those years, but this Bison Journey was particularly vivid. While I have never been certain of its exact meaning, when I opened the flap I understood I was setting my life on a course from which there was no turning back. Walking toward the teepee, I was fully aware that I didn't have to look inside. I could have turned around at any moment, walked away, been safe. But I had the notion that waiting inside was an energy, a potential as it were, and that it was mine.

Before opening the flap, I made a deliberate and conscious choice to see what was inside the teepee. Who knew where that decision would lead or what it would require of me? Certainly not I. My choice was a simple one—did I want the adventure?

I wanted the adventure.

A few weeks after taking the Bison Journey my life began to metamorphose. A longtime friend was dying of brain cancer and on her request, I flew to Carmel, California, to share a few last days together. The experience was emotionally exhausting and required my deepest awarenesses. However, it was on that same trip that I quite unexpectedly met a Canadian gentleman named David John Horrigan. Fond of scuba diving, sailing, and building things with wood, he worked on the San Diego waterfront as a marine engineer and lived in a world I knew absolutely nothing about. But something about him caught my attention.

Soon, I began to sense movement "behind the scenes" of my life, as if an invisible force was at work on my behalf. I trusted this perception and as each new pathway presented itself, I embraced it. One step led to another, the steps unfolded into a trail, the trail led into the future. The chance meeting with David turned into a love affair and the love affair turned into a marriage. Because of David, I moved from Denver to San Diego, which meant leaving my family of origin behind. That was extremely hard. But I ended up with a new family of my own. Because of the move, I changed jobs after thirteen years with the same company. It was frightening to say the least. But my new job is wonderful. During all this, I quit smoking and took up breathing. I gave my skis to a friend and learned to sail.

The months that followed the Bison Journey proved to be an incredible period of my life. I felt like a snake shedding its skin. As each familiar reality fell away, a new world took its place. And the new world seemed to more closely resemble my deepest dreams.

I think we all have these stories to tell. We have all lived through times when life accommodated our desires. But in order for that to happen, we had to first accept our particular experiences as real and then we had to have the courage to go forward into the new future, no matter what changes it brought.

Menopause is no different. If we want it to be a positive experience, if we want to make the Red Moon Passage, then we need to consciously choose the adventure. We need to let the bison out of our teepees.

In selecting the women for this book, I wanted someone who was a friend of the bison. I wanted someone who understood that "reality" was changeable. I wanted Professor Paula Gunn Allen.

Paula Gunn Allen is a jet-age Indian who lives by ancient traditions. She's both a mother and a daughter, author and reader, teacher and student. Aside from her many other accomplishments, Paula was one of the first people in the United States to receive a Ph.D. in Native American studies. Calling herself a "thought shaman," she jokes that her work is not healing physical ailments but healing ill *thoughts*.

Like several of the women in this book, I first met Paula through her writings. One rainy winter day, *Grandmothers of the Light* was sitting quietly on the shelf of the Lighthouse Bookstore in Mission Beach, California. It was one book among a thousand, but my attention was drawn to it. The title said it was "a source book for female shamans." I gently touched the cover. Could this woman teach me something? I wondered.

The answer was unequivocally yes.

It was in this book that Paula introduced me to the Laguna people's legendary Grandmother Spider, the dreamer of all life. Grandmother Spider, sometimes known as Thought Woman, "thought the earth, the sky, the galaxy and all that is into being and as she thinks, so we are."[1]

Grandmother Spider was and is the old woman of my vision. The myths about her are the myths that speak to the female power of creation. She is testament to the fact that our ability to give birth extends beyond the physical act of bearing children into the metaphysical realm of creating the universe.

In 1993, I unwittingly chose a day to talk with Paula, special envoy of Grandmother Spider, during which the moon (the oh so feminine moon) was 23,000 miles closer to the earth than normal, a fact I found both amusing and appropriate. As it is sometimes apt to do, the universe was creating poetry for me.

Paula understands the power of old women, both from an intellectual viewpoint and from personal experience. You might think what she has to say is esoteric, but her knowledge is not textbook knowledge that never gets applied in real life. It's knowledge that's lived and felt and spoken and slept and dreamed and laughed and cried. It originates from the spiritual realm and demonstrably works in our everyday universe.

As an example, Paula emerged out the other side of her own menopausal journey looking an amazing ten years younger and feeling physically and mentally healthier than she'd felt in a long time. This wasn't due to an unexplainable miracle and it was not a product of medical intervention. According to Paula, it was simply the result of living, underline *living,* ordinary life. Further, she says that menopause can and should be that way for everyone.

When I met her, Paula was on sabbatical from teaching at the University of California in Los Angeles. She had moved to Albuquerque, her place of origin, to complete two new books. In the spring of 1993, new family in tow, I traveled to New Mexico to seek her wisdom. Paula and I had a long conversation and talked of

[1] Allen, Paula Gunn. *Grandmothers of the Light,* Beacon Press, Boston, 1991, page 28.

many wonderful ideas that can help heal our minds and consequently our lives and the lives of those in our circle. She offered great insight into the menopausal journey.

It happened on one of those days where the sun washes the entire world in a glow of warm, golden light. I was glad to be in New Mexico because the land there has always felt spiritual to me. There are many places of power where if you stand still and open yourself to all possibilities, you can feel the healing energy and hear the ancient wisdom. This particular day felt ominous, like something special was going to happen.

As we sat in her living room drinking coffee, I reminded her that in her book *The Sacred Hoop* she made reference to the four stages of a woman's life according to Native American tradition. This concept has intrigued me since I first encountered it because it seems such a useful tool in understanding life and our relationship within it. Could we start there? I asked her. Could she talk about the four stages of life?

Paula laughed. "You hope I remember them, don't you?"

"Well, I brought your book with me just in case you don't," I told her, and she laughed again.

With a somewhat mischievous glint in her eye, Paula put down her coffee cup and drew a circle on a piece of paper, dividing it into four quadrants and labeling the lines North, East, South, and West, like a compass. "This is our medicine wheel," she told me. "This will help us understand the secrets of life."

And so, enter the thought shaman.

Paula Gunn Allen

THE FOUR STAGES OF LIFE

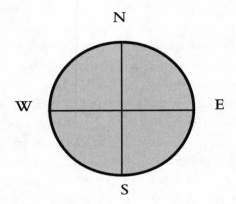

North to East, the first quadrant on the medicine wheel, is about birth to puberty, which is about ages one to thirteen. That's the period when we are just learning. Just learning whatever—walk, talk, think, cook, play, interact with other humans, everything.

The next period is from East to South. In the old times, a young woman would have her first menstrual period and then within a very short time, she would have her first child. So this period is about mothering. It's also about developing advanced social skills—not just nurturing your own family, but being very engaged in your community. At this level it would be your town, your neighborhood, your village, your city.

From South to West is a period of maturity. We would say that now the corn is ripe. It's harvest time. You begin to move beyond narrow personal concerns. When you are little, it's you and your family. Then when you're a mother, it's you and your community. Here you become concerned with your relationship to the larger world. During this time, people begin to study medicine ways. Maybe they are going to be politicians or maybe they are going to be nurturers, so they start accumulating grandchildren or finding young women to mentor. Whatever people do, the West represents a period of mastery of your life.

The last period in many ways is you, your true self. It's you and the great mystery combining, rendering a life into a meaning. As you move toward death you have to realign your relationship to the world and it isn't with just the living—your friends, your family, your cats and dogs, your horses, whatever—but rather it's your relationship to what you don't know, to the great beyond.

When people reach this period of their lives, they turn their thoughts, whether consciously or not and in whatever context is real for them, to matters of the spirit. In the native world, individual people have different ways of accommodating to this, but it's clear that the movement now is toward winter (North) and everything gets very quiet.

Now, menopause—defined as the cessation of menstruation and including all the hormone storms that go on prior to the cessation—happens on the cusp of the third and fourth quadrants. It marks that exact bridge. The change of life *is* the change of quadrants.

A woman on the West/North cusp, a woman moving from the third quadrant to the fourth, should know that she is entering a period of life in which contemplation of the mysteries of the universe is normal and perhaps even necessary if she is to stay in balance.

THE MENOPAUSAL CONSCIOUSNESS

For the Lakota and for many tribal people, the West is the area of psychic phenomena whereas North is the place of wisdom and purity of the inner self. Going from West to North is going from the psychic storm to the quiet and meditative calm of winter. If you remember this while in the midst of a hormone storm, you can better understand the event for what it is.

I would caution women in their twenties and early thirties to be very thoughtful before becoming too involved with these psychic energies. But if you are in your late forties or early fifties, I suspect it's entirely natural. As the bleeding stops the fire goes within. At this point, if you have handled the energy properly, it begins to generalize throughout the whole cellular and neuromuscular system and you will have psychic phenomena.

Much of this is reminiscent of puberty. My guess is that the paranormal is somehow hooked into hormonal balances and dynamics. During the period of menopause, you are in a state when you are sacred, just as in pregnancy, particularly early pregnancy, and at puberty and to a lesser extent during your monthly period.

Women are "different" during these times. Being in a sacred state means that you are open or porous and because of that, energies from the nonphysical world can permeate your consciousness, including your hands and your feet. Consciousness is not just in your mind as so many people think; it involves the entire body. Full consciousness is within yourself, in your nervous system and your endocrine system.

There is a mystical power to the endocrine system and a woman can learn to control it. I don't want to sound too patriarchal, but you can learn to ride those currents like a hawk rides the wind, and use them as perceptual modes.

When students of mine have been either just premenopausal or postmenopausal, they do the most interesting thing with information. The information goes in at the brain level—the writing notes with hands and eyes and ears. But when it comes back out on a test or in a journal, it has been completely integrated with life experiences. It does not come out as segregated information, but instead

it is integrated with "what my girlfriend told me" or "I was walking up the street to do my grocery shopping."

I think this integration is probably the most important aspect
of mature consciousness, which begins to show at menopause. And
this is why medicine women do not practice until they have
reached their menopausal years.

SUCCESSFUL PASSAGE

In order to make the passage through menopause successfully,
women need to be aware of what is happening to them. In the
same manner that a young girl might be frightened if she doesn't
understand why there is suddenly blood between her legs, an older
woman can be frightened if she doesn't understand the menopausal
phenomenon. After menopause, the balance between intellect,
thought, emotion, and spirit is deeply harmonized and yet quite in-
tense, and thus profound.

The power acquired by this particular balance can be used for
helping another person, for healing communities, for learning and
growing, or it can be seen as an affliction. But if you see it that way,
it will turn on you. It will afflict you.

Like the four stages of life, you can put this on a wheel. East is
knowledge—data, information, CNN, nonfiction book, magazine
article. South is nurturing, loving, connecting, bonding. West is
where I live with my inner self and connect with the great mysteries that surround my normal life and permeate it, and North is wisdom, the place where everything is integrated.

FEMALE BODIES, MENOPAUSAL BODIES

Our bodies are going to change when all this happens. If you are
an older woman, your body is just not going to work like a younger

woman's. And I want to say for all women, our bodies have never worked like men's. One of the biggest mistakes modern women make—and it's because they have been coerced into it—is that they keep using male models of spirituality. Whether it's Christian, Buddhist, or New Age, all of these models are about how *men* integrate their immortal self with their mortal self.

Men have a different physiology and their methods are designed to work for that physiology, not for the physiology of women. We are really different kinds of beings and so we need different kinds of things to stay in balance and to stay clear and to grow without doing damage to ourselves. You can ruin your endocrine system and you can ruin your nervous system. You can, for example, create so much damage that you have severe PMS. And if you have severe PMS, it's your body telling you that you are not doing it right. PMS is not a medical condition. It's a spiritual condition.

But I don't mean that you are being punished. It's just that your vehicle is very intelligent and she will tell you, "Hey wait a minute."

If you live in America, you subconsciously identify with male models. You don't even know that you are doing it, because you've been trained from first grade on to do that. But you are screwing up your system. Once again, it's not a *fault*. Women simply haven't been given any alternatives. They haven't been taught what "female" really looks like.

Female doesn't look like male and it doesn't look like "hysterical, flighty, and dumb." Those models are not going to work. If we follow them, we are going to have PMS because both are inappropriate to true female consciousness, which is integrally physiological, psychological, and spiritual. That's why a woman can go through menopause in ways that are extraordinarily painful and frightening. Because the farther out of balance you've gotten with your female harmonies, never mind your individual ones, the more the damage keeps accumulating. It keeps getting worse.

So it's very important to live in balance, to engage in your femininity, your womanness.

THE SACRED HOOP

When I was growing up, my mother used to say, "All life is a circle and everything has its place within it." Sometimes she would say this as an admonition. It wasn't a kind, gentle, nurturing kind of statement, you understand. She was reminding me of my duty. It was straighten up, act right.

One time I got in a robin's nest where there were babies. Mother caught me and she was very upset. She explained that the bird mother would never go back because the smell of my hands would be on the babies.

She used to say this same thing to my father. He had "a poor attitude toward snakes," meaning he didn't like them. But mother kept a resident bull snake under the house anyway, and she wouldn't let anybody near it, including him. Her excuse was that the snake ate the mice and there were too many mice. But the underlying belief was that "all life is a circle and everything has its place within it."

What my mother was talking about was the same belief as the Sioux tradition of the Sacred Hoop. But the Sacred Hoop is more than just the verbalization of the idea that "everything is connected." The concept of the Sacred Hoop contains a philosophy for correct living *because* everything is connected.

In my book *The Sacred Hoop* I translated an ancient Keres song:

> *I add my breath to your breath*
> *That our days may be long on the Earth*
> *That the days of our people may be long*
> *That we may be one person*
> *That we may finish our roads together*

May our mother bless you with life
May our Life Paths be fulfilled.

Breath is life, and the intermingling of breath is the purpose of good living. This is in essence the great principle on which all productive living must rest, for relationships among all the beings of the universe must be fulfilled; in this way each individual life may also be fulfilled.[2]

If all of life is a circle and everything has its place and relationship within, then menopausal women have a place within that great hoop of being and they have relationships to everything else within the circle. You don't leave the circle when you go through menopause. There isn't one circle for women ages fifteen to thirty-nine and another for women over forty. So the thinking that says passing through menopause somehow puts one outside the realm of dynamic or purposeful life is destructive and contrary to the natural order of things. But living within the circle demands that we take our place. It demands that we choose our right relationship to all that is.

MYTH AS TEACHER

In seeking correct relationships, the ancient myths can help us. Paula wrote one of the best descriptions of what myth is and how myth can enrich our lives that I have ever read. She wrote:

Myth functions as an affirmation of self that transcends the temporal. It guides our attention toward a view of ourselves, a possibility, that we might not otherwise encounter. It shows us our own

[2] Allen, Paula Gunn. *The Sacred Hoop*, Beacon Press, Boston, 1986, page 56.

*ability to accept and allow the eternal to be part of our selves. . . .
Thus myth shows us that it is possible to relate ourselves to the
grand and mysterious universe that surrounds and informs our being; it makes us aware of other orders of reality and experience and
in that awareness makes the universe our home. It is magic.*[3]

I believe that one of the greatest teaching myths is that of Thought
Woman or Grandmother Spider. Here is the beginning of the legend of
Grandmother Spider from Paula's book, Grandmothers of the Light.

*Ooma-oo, long ago. The Spider was in place where only she was.
There was no light or dark, there was no warm wind, no rain or
thunder. There was no cold, no ice or snow. There was only the
Spider. She was a great wise woman whose powers were beyond
imagining. . . . Her power is complete and total. It is pure and
cleaner than the void. It is the power of thought, we say, but not
the kind of thought people do all the time. It's like the power of a
dream but more pure. Like the spirit of vision, but more clear. It
has no shape or movement because it just is. It is the power that
creates all that is and it is the power of all that is.*

*In that place where she was alone and complete with her
power, she thought about her power, how it sang to her, how she
dreamed from it, how she wished to have someone to share the
songdream with her. . . . So she thought to the power once and
knew a rippling, a wrinkling within. Then she knew she was old,
and wrinkled, and that the power's first song was a song of great
age. She named that place Northwest.*[4]

I love Grandmother Spider. She is one of my favorite beings and she
comes from many different traditions. The Hopi Indians have their version.

[3] Allen, *The Sacred Hoop*, pages 116, 117.
[4] Allen, *Grandmothers of the Light*, pages 34, 35.

*In the Beginning there were only two: Tawa, the Sun God, and
Spider Woman, the Earth Goddess. All the mysteries and power
in the Above belonged to Tawa, while Spider Woman controlled the
magic of Below. In the Underworld, adobe of the gods, they dwelt
and they were All. There was neither man nor woman, bird nor
beast, no living thing until these Two willed it to be.[5]*

*Navajo mythology also contains stories of Spider Woman, one of which
says, "Spider Woman instructed the Navajo women how to weave on a loom
which Spider Man told them how to make."[6] Many of the Navajo Spider
Women stories talk of how Spider Woman simply is their consciousness.*

*Bearing in mind the great legacy of Spider Woman, I asked Paula to
talk specifically about her and what secrets she can reveal to menopausal
women.*

According to Keres tradition, Grandmother Spider, Thought
Woman, is the creatrix of our world. The Laguna people say that as
she thinks, so we are. She thinks everything to be as it is—every relationship, every connection. You might think of her thoughts as
the Sacred Hoop. She is, or the mind of Thought Woman is, that
place where everything is connected with everything.

I say we are her dream, but I have to make a caution here.
Dream in the Indian mystical, metaphysical system doesn't mean
the same thing as it means in the white world. In the white world,
dream means you go to sleep and you have a dream. In the Indian
world, as one man put it, "It's hard to tell the difference with these
old Indians between when they are talking about a dream and
when they are talking about reality." You see, we don't draw lines.

[5] Mullett, C. M. *Spider Woman Stories: Legends of the Hopi Indians,* University of Arizona Press, Tucson, 1991, page 1.
[6] Locke, Raymond Friday. *Sweet Salt: Navajo Folktales and Mythology,* Roundtable
Publishing, Santa Monica, 1990, page 199.

It's like Laotse—"I don't know if I was a butterfly dreaming I was a man, or am a man dreaming I was a butterfly."

Grandmother Spider, Thought Woman, dreams in the sense of the shaman or a sorceress or an incredibly adept Druid. She literally creates out of nothing, something. She's the creator god. She's our analog to the Middle Eastern concept of how things go. Only "He" makes a clay model—Adam. She makes a thought.

THOUGHT THAT CREATES

In order to accomplish the level of thought that creates, we have to learn to think differently. It's not the verbalizations we do in our head. In my spiritual classes, I used to call that the blather machine. You know, blah, blah, blah. That's all conditioning. It's useless. We all do it and I don't mean stop doing it, because you can't stop doing it. But you can stop accepting it as being meaningful. There's a deeper way to think that they call meditation in the Buddhist and New Age worlds. That gets closer to the kind of thinking that I'm referring to, but again, it is *not* meditation, visualization, or doing affirmations.

Two or three times in my life I have made a commitment, a decision, that I call "to my toes." There's a particular psychological or psychosomatic state that goes with such a decision, and when I've decided *in that state*, everything has changed.

But owning up to this kind of power is very difficult for women. We are much more comfortable in assigning those abilities to men or to gods. One of the things I notice with my students in my spiritual school and also at the university, is that women in America are deeply conditioned—it's even worse in England—to *not* think. It's not that they can't. It's that a barrier was established in early schooling, if not in the home. But it's very dangerous to the whole world right now because we have to think. It's very important. WE. WOMEN. HAVE. TO. THINK.

This means that you notice your emotional condition and you notice the psychic state you're in. Today I woke up sort of blah, not happy and not sad. There's a grouchiness off in the distance. I need to know that because it's going to color my whole day. Everything that I do and everything I see, perceive, and hear I am going to interpret through that screen.

A woman has to know these things. You have to know "I'm angry, I'm sad, I'm glad, I'm scared," whatever. That's your emotional condition. Actually, it's not emotional. It's the endocrine system. It's just chemicals in your bloodstream, but you need to know it. You need to know what impressions you are bringing in. For instance, we are having this conversation about Thought Woman. That's an impression. My mind, my thought part, is very engaged right now in the whole concept of this great mystery that is Thought Woman. Then at the same time, I have to pee and I want some more coffee and I'm thirsty and I've got this physiological stuff going on. In a larger sense I'm postmenopausal. That means should I take estrogen replacement therapy? And I'm losing weight, which means everything is sagging and I'm going to look ugly.

All of these things are happening and I can integrate them. That's what the Dream with a capital *D* is. All of these states become dynamically interconnected. You don't try to shove some of them away. You try to bring them all into play in a balanced way simultaneously. And wham, the thought begins to germinate. It begins to grow. And that's how you do it.

WASHING THE DISHES

By the way, sitting and meditating is a bad idea for women's physiology. It's a very bad idea. I've looked and looked, and I can't find a trace of any native practice where women meditate that way. And I cannot find any native system where people don't eat meat and fish.

Sitting meditation and being a vegetarian are both Aryan patriarchal concepts. They come from that race of people who gave us the "Father" god. We can't dream the Grandmother's dream if we stay hooked into the Father's dream. It can't be done.

One of the problems here is that we are dealing with Middle Eastern thought. Christianity is a Middle Eastern religion, as is Judaism and Islam, and possibly Hinduism in its Buddhist form. Read what Marija Gimbutas has to say in *The Language of the Goddess*.[7] If you look back at the origin of Western civilization, it starts in the Black Sea region in the Caucasus area and it is inevitably patriarchal. Inevitably the father—it would become grandfather and even great grandfather—is the head of the clan, and the women, children, and cattle are possessions. It's hierarchical and exclusive.

We have to integrate the Father's dream, because we were raised in it. We can't just banish it. But to heal, we have to understand that the Father is not Jesus the Son of Mary. He's the Grandmother's grandson. It's his Grandmother who is Thought Woman, and it's her thought that holds, guides, and empowers him. Besides, he is twin brothers; he is "they."

In tribal thought, the same icon will be called female by the women and male by the men. I thought the Kiowa had a Grandmother Bundle.[8] But the reason I thought that was because the women who wrote about it had been talking to the women. Later I heard a male scholar talk about the Grandfather Bundle and it

[7] Gimbutas, Marija. *The Language of the Goddess*, Harper & Row, San Francisco, 1989.

[8] The term Grandmother Bundle refers to a medicine bundle as used by Kiowa. My first encounter with this term was in *Black Elk: The Sacred Ways of the Lakota* by Wallace Black Elk, HarperCollins, San Francisco, 1990, page 86. "So that spirit told us in the longhouse about those sacred bundles the longhouse people had hanging in there. One bundle had a Chanunpa (Sacred Pipe) in it, one had a whistle, and one had a medicine in it."

took quite a bit of his lecture before I realized, "Oh, they are talking about the same medicine bundle."

The point is that male rituals are suitable for the male anatomy and consciousness and female rituals are suitable for the female. When they come together, which they often do, the female part enhances female consciousness and the male part enhances male consciousness.

So instead of sitting meditation, women should wash the dishes.

This really annoys modern women because feminine consciousness, the tremendous power of female thought, is so disstatused in our world. They say washing the dishes is trivial. Everything that is associated with the feminine is trivialized. They trivialize it so that we won't use our power. And it works, doesn't it?

Women under sixty don't want to do things like wash the dishes because they don't want to be insignificant and useless. They don't want to end up like so many women you see in nursing homes who are senile and incapable of leading meaningful lives. I understand that. I don't want that either. But that's not built into female consciousness, especially Grandmother consciousness. That is built into the devaluation of female thought. What causes diminishment is the devaluation, not the thought, and not the dishes.

So you have to do the dishes. Sweep the floors. Adopt some grandchildren or become a politician. It depends on your mode. Going off, retreating, and becoming a medicine person is also a possibility. But what's important is that you are integrated along the lines of your physiology.

ACROSS THE GREAT DIVIDE

When women don't have the coping mechanisms to handle the depression that can accompany menopause, they usually turn to their doctors. And all too often, the doctors recommend drugs. But drugs cover up and deny, they don't heal. If you connect with your depression and deal with it spiritually you can transform. But you will never make the passage if you make the experience inaccessible. This is one of the reasons I have been searching for rituals that might help menopausal women connect with their unconscious and deal with these forces. During our conversation, I asked Paula about such rites of passage, and in typical fashion she managed to change my fundamental concept of what ritual is.

When you get up in the morning there are two things you can do, and you can do these if you are a Christian or a nonbeliever or a Native American or Jewess. One is to be quiet for a little bit. Just listen. Not to yourself. Just listen. Usually listen is a transitive verb as in "listen to what?" No. No. No "to what?" Just listen. I lie there for a little while before I get out of the bed and I just let it be. Right there I get connected. It helps me stay with me.

The other is that you can pray. Go outside and make an offering. Cornmeal is a wonderful thing to use. Just blow it toward the sun and say, "Thank you. I am here again today. Thank you." You go through your entire day—and this is hard to remember because of how we live—and every time you do remember, check back in to yourself and say thank you.

I think: "I am really lucky." It helps. In the pueblos they say that your obligation is to think good thoughts—always—because if you don't think good thoughts, it won't rain and then everybody will starve and it will be your fault. What a responsibility! But just that idea—keeping connected with the world around you—helps you understand that you are part of the world because of the character of what you think.

To me, ritual is what goes on all the time, waking and sleeping. You respect what's around you. You vacuum the floor because you respect possessions. You get the carpet cleaned or the upholstery done or wear clean clothes because it's about honoring life and honoring the gifts that you have been given. It's an inner thing. But that is what ritual is.

Ritual is about making outward expressions of inner states. And like a feedback loop, if I respect my surroundings then they nurture me because I am nurturing myself by respecting them, and it begins to generalize.

Burning incense as a ritual to clean the air of any negative psychic vibrations is another possibility. I know when I'm depressed I start filling my space with negativity and the minute I walk in the door it smacks me in the face. It's all my negative thoughts. So that's why I said do the dishes. If you keep the place clean—physically dust, wash, whatever—that negativity decreases. And that's psychic. It looks physical but it's actually psychic and spiritual.

THE GREAT DIVIDE

It's absolutely amazing what happened to my consciousness as I crossed the Great Divide. My mind cleared up. I didn't know it would be like that. I didn't know I would feel better. Older women, including my mother, kept telling me, "You will really feel good once you are past fifty, once you've passed menopause." And this is true. It's amazing how beautifully your mind works.

I've met women in their eighties and nineties who started new careers, traveling all over the world, not as somebody's widow but as active participants in their world. To a certain extent that means you must take care of yourself so your body doesn't fall apart because it's easier for it to fall apart after menopause than before. But you don't have to be condemned to sickness.

I started into menopause when I was thirty-two or thirty-three. When I was having hot flashes, it was miserable, and I had these emotional storms that were reminiscent of being fourteen. By the time I was thirty-five, I couldn't walk up a flight of stairs. I was very ill. I was dying. I don't know how I worked, how I functioned, how I wrote. It was a nightmare. The years went by and I was sick, I was sick, I was sick.

Before my periods stopped, I was diagnosed with chronic fatigue syndrome, which led me eventually to acupuncture. So I was doing acupuncture and Chinese herbs, and approaching the cessation of my periods. Then, when I was nearing fifty, I made a fundamental to-my-toes decision—no more abuse. There will be no more abuse in my life.

I think all these things go together. I became aware that I had to take better care of myself. But in trying to learn how to take care of me, I discovered that I didn't even know what "me" meant. Somebody would say, "What do you need?" and I didn't have a clue. What happened is that I began to learn the difference between need and want. Which doesn't mean I can't want. It's just that I didn't do anything about my own *needs* because I didn't know wanting and needing were different.

Somewhere in there, I remember my mother saying, "I think you will feel much better after you go through the change." I filed it away because I didn't know if the disease had any relationship to this long menopausal process. But the change of life is not the day your period stops. For many women the symptoms go on for twenty years.

My periods finally stopped sometime in the past three or four years. But before they stopped, my energy level began to increase and I began to feel much much better.

ON THE VOICE
AND THE SILENCE OF AGE

Aside from coping with the physiological changes of menopause, there's also this bizarre having to come to terms with being an old woman. That's very difficult. It's just not part of how you think of yourself all the days of your life.

I have to confront it when I look in the mirror, and I also have to confront it when I am the recipient of other people's negative opinions about my age. The hard part is spending Christmas at your children's. They and their friends think of you as "the mother" or "the mother-in-law." Remember how you related to your mother and your friends' mothers when you were thirty? You thought they were old. Well, you feel this coming at *you*.

And everybody calls you madame. People assume that because I am an aging woman, I must be a dimwit. I'm not a sexual object anymore, so I have no identity. This is extremely difficult for me because I want to have an identity. Yes, I'm a writer and, yes, I'm famous, but that doesn't work when you are at Wal-Mart. It doesn't work when you go to the bank to open an account. And it isn't just the young men that do this to you. It's the young women as well. And this is part of what we need to heal.

As a younger woman, you're objectified. Somebody's always hitting on you. But at least your boobs were there, if you know what I mean. Some part of you was in the room. But now, I'm not in the room at all. I just disappear. It's very hard. That's the downside.

The upside is that I can say anything I want to anybody. So now I get up in front of groups and out it comes. I remember years ago when I had just reached forty, my grandmother said, "Now that you are an old woman, you have to tell them." For Native American women, permission comes with age. Permission and an obligation to say as much of the truth as you see it, whatever it might be. You must speak up. You have to *say*. Because you are the one who knows.

So that helps me. That's a good thing. I don't feel pushed into silence. I feel pushed into voice by the aging.

And there is also tremendous power of the spiritual or paranormal in being invisible. Grandmother Spider is very small. You can't see her. Silence and invisibility put you in the borderlands, or as an anthropologist would call it, in a liminal state, which is where all the real power is. It's not status. It's the power to transform. The power of magic. You don't get that from visibility. The more visible you become the less of that power you can access.

If you have a lot of visibility it's harder to be generative because you are hemmed in and hedged in, in so many ways. But some people need to work on illuminating the silence because there's a sense that if you are invisible, you are not entitled to good health care, you're not entitled to a decent standard of living, and, above all, you are not entitled to dignity. I'm sure that's wrong on every level. But on the other hand, other people need to be and work in the silence and protect and defend that.

A balanced truth has everything in it. Modern people who are not grown up have the idea that there is only one way and if I could only find the right one way then we could make everybody do it and then we would all live happily ever after. That's not right. The planet is infinite. Mother Earth, the mother creator, loves the act of creation. She never does anything in ones. I know that multiplicity—a lot of everything—is the proper model for how we need to go about addressing our lives and our planet in this era. We've got to get over what I think of as fundamentalist thought, which is that there is only one way. Because there's not. There are as many ways as there are creatures on the planet.

So personally, I won't shut up. But I treasure my silence and my solitude as well. I need both things.

STORIES ABOUT MENOPAUSE

There are lots and lots and lots of Native American stories about old women. One of the things I love about the oral tradition is that everybody's in it. Kids and young women who are first having babies and mothers and fathers and grandfathers and lovers and suicides and heroes and warrioresses and warriors. You find every possible way of interpreting experience in reality and every possible way also means age groups and gender groups. But at this period of my life, I'm happiest with the grandmother stories because I'm a grandmother and I identify. It helps me explore my reality. It gives me things to think about as I go through my day-to-day life.

There's the wise old grandmother and the foolish grandmother and there's the mean and angry grandmother. There's the ogre woman. I like Grandmother Spider, Thought Woman, who thinks the world into being. I like Grandmother of the Light, Xmucane, the Mayan goddess who created everybody. Xmucane tried to make beings that would satisfy all the other gods. After many attempts, she finally succeeded, and this is how the human race was born. Then there's a wonderful Grandmother Sky Woman among the Anishnake and Haudenesaunee. Grandmother Sky Woman created the human world after she fell through the void of space.

After a lot of research into other traditions, I concluded that it was all so simple. The stories are told over and over again. There were always women, sometimes two, sometimes three, sometimes more—and they did it. They were great sorceresses, divine shamans. They brought life to the planet, they became the planet.

This is the power of feminine and especially of Grandmother.

MENOPAUSE AND MOTHER EARTH

This is the time. Look at Jose Arguelles's book, *The Mayan Factor*. It concerns the change of life for the planet. But the part he didn't say, because he didn't know, is that it's about the return of the Grandmothers.

What's happening with our planet right now—all the turmoil, all the shifting in consciousness that's going on—is because Grandmother energy is getting more and more palatable. That's why you are seeing so many older women suddenly popping up in public life, beginning with Golda Meir and Indira Gandhi. They were the first swallows of spring. Slowly, we are seeing the flowering of female consciousness in the Grandmother age. Female wisdom, or what I call gynosophy, is the wisdom of women. But it's *old* women.

The reason females are getting more visible has to do with this ray or this force or this power. It's getting stronger and stronger. Other people who are not Grandmothers want to hear. Their consciousness is attuning to that frequency, as ours is. We are carriers of her dream. I'm not doing it. I'm just an automobile that she drives in. I have my own life. But that's different from my work as Paula Gunn Allen.

All this is menopause. We are going through the change and becoming Grandmothers and the planet is also becoming a Grandmother.

Menopause is a liminal state, which means it's dangerous. But what's on the other side of the divide is unbelievable. I know that for sure because I've crossed the divide. So I know that right now for the planet it's hot flashes and cold wars, depressive states, all this stuff. Also a lot of new ideas, a lot of chaos, and this emotional roller coaster and intellectual confusion. This babble of voices. All of that is part of this tremendous process. And she's going to wake up one of these mornings a postmenopausal lady and she's going to say, "Oh, I'm Grandma." And we will be okay.

THE MENOPAUSAL SHAMAN

I'm a different kind of shaman. I'm a thought shaman. When I first got my Ph.D. somebody said to me, "I tell everybody you are a doctor and they want to know what your specialty is." And I said, "Oh, I doctor sick thought." And this is the truth. This is what I do.

Let me play professor here for a minute. My theory is that there's a way without feathers and drums and incense, and even dancing, that is much better than feathers and drums. Those are things that help you focus, but they aren't it. By the way, women dance (I mean dance as in Native American dances—what you call ceremonies), and men drum. Men have to sit still. Nothing gets through to them unless they sit still (though, of course, men dance, too). But women integrate. That's why we have to move. That's why you have to do the dishes or go dancing. It will work.

There is a level that is more inclusive, that is pure thought, which properly would be called intuition. And that's where the actual transformation is occurring. So my shamanic work doesn't look like what is thought of as shamanic work in New Age circles today.

My work is that I live in a suburban apartment and I've got three TV sets. Those are my magic fires. And I am very engaged in using my deep thought to effect changes in the thinking system of the people who run the planet. Because if we can change the way we think—not our political opinions and our political correctness but our deep, deep values and assumptions—if we can transform that, then the whole thing will transform.

I've never publicly told this to anyone, but I will tell you. I had a vision years and years ago. I was a young woman then and I still had visions. Now I can't tell the difference. But some man came and took me on a boat among the stars. He showed me how he could reach in with his hand and touch the star in such a way that he changed the thought that the star was having. He said, "That's what a poet does. That's a poet." Then we came back to the planet and I tried it a couple of times with a few people I knew. There was this thing around their head where the thoughts lived. Maybe it's the astral body, but I don't think so. It's probably the thought body, the mental body. If you reached in a certain way—you didn't exactly touch, you just put your finger near it—it was like a magnetic hole, and if you had a particular intention or vision or sense, it would transmit and the stuff would reorganize. Everything would recalibrate within the hoop of thought.

That's a way of picturing what I do.

FINAL ADVICE

There's some wonderful grandmotherly advice that I got from Louise Hay. You say to yourself at least seven hundred times a day, "I love and approve of myself exactly the way I am." And if I had absolutely nothing else that I could teach, if I had one sound bite, that's the one. The Lagunas would call that thinking good thoughts.

It will transform your life.

PART SIX

Alchemy and the Imagery of Menopause

DREAM GARDEN

I slip through gossamer membranes
down and down into
the mulched soul space of the garden.
There I find the bulbs and seeds of self.
Dormant. Unattended.
It is high time to water and make fertile and caress
that inviolate core of my being
else I wither into my old woman's skin.

—Jeanne Achterberg

This much we know. Menopause is a process. It is not a singular, isolated event and it does not happen out of context with the rest of our lives. It is mythic in that it happens to everyone and it is personal in that it happens to you. It is also more likely to take ten years than one minute, and more liable to cause a series of small sparks rather than one big explosion.

One other possibility we now understand is that if one embraces the biological, emotional, mental, and spiritual transformations available in the experience, menopause can become an initiatory rite of passage into a new realm of being. Wise women aren't born, they are formed out of the processes of life.

This section is about some of those processes and a particular wise woman I call the Alchemist.

This story begins in the beginning of my search for the Wise Woman archetype. At first it seemed that this archetype belonged strictly to the world of the intellect rather than the world of breath. She was myth, she was legend, she was fairy tale, she was vision. But she was not flesh and blood. I was in error, however, and soon found out that she lives in this realm and wears many faces.

While the Wise Woman/Changing Woman/Grandmother Spider has not yet become part of the mass consciousness, part of our everyday thinking, I believe our culture, thankfully, is headed in that direction. When I opened to the possibility of the Wise Woman, when I made a space for her in my inner consciousness, one by one the women in this book appeared in my outer life. And when I asked them for help in the menopausal journey, they graciously and in the manner of the Wise Woman archetype turned in my direction and offered a hand. "Come this way," they said, and with each little step, my middle-aged life began to transform.

Somewhere in this process, my awareness of the connectivity of the universe moved from my mind to my body. It stopped being an idea I intellectually subscribed to and became a force I experienced. One of the accompanying realizations to this new awareness is that everything a person does, and I mean *everything*, matters.

You see, once you understand connectivity, you can never think of life in the same way. My previous conceptualization involved creation as cause and effect. In this model, the creative or destructive force causes a reaction in a nonempowered object/ entity that has no control over or responsibility for the force or the change it is experiencing. Now, four years into the transformation, my understanding is that things are drawn together or pulled apart because of connections—connections that each of us are creating or breaking with every thought we have and every action we take.

I must add a caution here that life is never strictly black and white, never simple, never one-sided, never absolute. Not all actions are equal. Not all thoughts have the same power. There are levels of being, layers of consciousness, and other realities. But with this in mind, we can look at the broad patterns as patterns and gain a better understanding of how life works.

Some of our actions/thoughts arise from the conscious realm. We are aware of what we do and how we feel. More than likely, we are also aware of the relationships and connections these actions/thoughts bring to our lives. Some of our actions/thoughts come forth from the unconscious realm. We may not be aware of these deeper motives, these imbedded patterns and ideas that silently rule our lives. But even though we are not aware of them, they are still *our* actions, *our* thoughts, *our* connections. They still affect our circle of being. This is important to understand. Your life is your life and it is not created by someone or something else. The challenge, of course, is to bring that which is unconscious into consciousness. We need to own the entirety of our selves and we need to operate at all levels. This is what growth is. This is what real maturity is all about.

The closer you are to the core of your being, the more you live from that place in concert with the truths that are yours, the stronger your connections will be and the more synchronicity you will experience in your life.

We cannot know the full consequences of our actions or exactly where our decisions and connections will take us. But what we can know is that life grows out of itself. We can know that our thoughts and actions have an effect. They matter.

I am fully aware that Jeanne Achterberg, Ph.D., appeared in my life because of the magic of transformation and the magic of connection. I do not believe that I could have or would have ever met her had I not traveled down certain roads or made an effort to live in certain ways. Let me explain.

I am employed by the American Association of Critical-Care

Nurses as the director of their publishing center. What that means on a practical level is that I am responsible, along with a team of eleven, for publishing their professional nursing journals. One morning while driving the fifty miles I drive each day to the office, I was considering my contribution to society. I'd taken up space and consumed my share of consumable things, but what had I actually given back that was of lasting value? I had no doubt made some contribution simply by working and not being a delinquent on the streets, and I had certainly made some contribution by doing my particular job well and helping to provide education materials for the art and science of nursing, but I was painfully aware that I was capable of contributing more. I was not fully engaged. I was not using my deepest abilities. This made me sad and seemed to be the source of the emptiness I sometimes felt. In an effort to resolve the situation, I did what I usually do. I took a journey to the other world and sent out a prayer. "I would like to be more useful, please," I told my friends over there.

And so the tribal drums began to beat. A remarkable series of events happened after this that I see as linked, as flowing out of the same well and rising from the same connections.

Now, I am fortunate in that, throughout my life, I have had good teachers. In the business world one of my teachers has been, and is, Sarah Sanford, the CEO of our company. She taught me something very valuable. She taught me to give an idea away. We have a rule at our office that once an idea is voiced, it then belongs to the group so that others may contribute to it, feed it, help it to grow. No one person *owns* an idea or a project. The work we do is teamwork, and every member of the team is important. And I believe it is this rule that is responsible for so much of our organization's success.

Shortly after my prayer was sent forth, in a conversation with Sarah, I briefly mentioned a thought that had recently entered my consciousness concerning a new medical journal. It wasn't even an idea yet, it was really more of a question. But she turned around, added to it, and mentioned it to our board of directors and our staff leadership team. The conversation grew. Other people talked about it, embraced it, contributed to it, passed it on. As the conversation continued to grow, the world began to change. And what happened in my life and what ultimately happened in the lives of others was that this new medical journal was born.

Except it wasn't your normal, toe-the-party-line medical journal. In fact, it was a renegade.

The journal is called *Alternative Therapies in Health and Medicine.* It is one of the few health-care journals that acknowledges spirit and the spiritual aspects of life as being equally real to the world of blood and bones and molecules. The editorial content focuses on nonconventional and cross-cultural medical treatments that have proven merit and promotes a deeper, more inclusive way of thinking about ourselves and our health. I love the journal because it encourages inquiry and honest search and research into the nature of the universe and our interaction with it.

It was in the process of birthing this journal that I met Jeanne. Because of my connections. Because of her connections. Because when the pupil is ready for the teacher, and the teacher is ready for the pupil, then the teacher and the pupil suddenly find themselves walking down the road together.

In the spring of 1993, a small meeting was set up at the Hilton in Santa Fe, New Mexico, to discuss how we might best proceed with the new publishing venture. A few key people, whom we'd never met but who had recently entered into our waking awareness, were invited. On the way to the meeting, Jeanne and I passed each other in the lobby. "Are you Bonnie?" "Are you Jeanne?" we asked, inquiring about that which we already knew.

Jeanne is a scientist, specifically she is a research psychologist, and what she studies is the impact of the spirit and human mind on life in general and health in particular. I call her the Alchemist because she has successfully used mind–body medicine to initiate transformation of the physical through employment of the spiritual.

One of the healing tools Jeanne uses is imagery, the natural human capacity for imagination. Imagery of this sort involves using one's ability to see or sense images that arise in our consciousness, as well as the ability to construct images willfully. The human body actually responds to images better than it responds to language. Because of this, imagery is a successful way of communicating with the physical aspects of ourselves.[1]

Try it. First tell yourself out loud that you are cold. Next, without words, simply imagine that you are walking down an icy city street in zero-degree weather with the wind whipping at your face. I don't need to say more.

As Jeanne told me, "The body and the mind are connected through the imagination. Images are the vehicle through which our mental processes reach deep into our cellular structures and communicate. They are the interface between what is deep within the cells of our bodies and what is deep within our psyche. Imagery, which is thought without words, can actually alter the intelligence of the cell."

Twenty years ago, Jeanne was one of the first scientists to step off the path of conventional medicine and use this knowledge in American hospitals. Her healing work with burn and cancer patients and others struggling with terminal disease has since gained national attention.

Jeanne is a professor at the Saybrook Institute in San Francisco, where she teaches at the doctoral level. I have the good fortune to speak with her frequently. Most of the time we talk about business, about the journal, because she is now the senior editor and I am

[1] From *Rituals of Healing* by Jeanne Achterberg, Ph.D.; Barbara Dossey, RN, MS; and Leslie Kolkmeier, RN, M.Ed. Bantam, New York, 1994.

now the publisher. But the rest of the time we talk about magic, about alchemy, about spirit and dreams and manifestation and the different realms of consciousness, and what we can do with all that in the context of our ordinary lives.

I met Jeanne in San Francisco one weekend and we talked for an entire day about midlife and menopause. Later, I had the following dream about her: Jeanne and I were having a conversation in which she was explaining to me why we couldn't use all of the twenty-five realms of magic. The reasons were cultural, she said. There were laws and taboos, and history taught us to be cautious. During the course of this conversation, both of us were suffocating. The air was so thick with pollution we could hardly breathe. Then for some strange reason, we decided that regardless of the risk we were going to embrace all twenty-five realms. At that point everything in the dream changed. The air became clear and we could breathe again. Rivers began to flow, a breeze rose up, and throughout the universe, planets that hadn't revolved in eons began to rotate once again.

This is Jeanne's work. This is her alchemy. This is why I chose her to speak through my book. We all need to stop suffocating. We all need to breathe deeply and be whole again and to live our lives to the fullest potential. And as Jeanne tells us, we can start by listening.

༺ *Jeanne Achterberg* ༻

IMAGERY

The easiest way to define imagery is that it's thought using the senses. It's not making pictures in your head and it's not imagining cancer cells being eaten up by white blood cells. It's essentially a thought process that is without words and probably very primitive.

Everyone has images. They are basic to the human mind. The more we learn about imagery, the more we realize that it seems to be the interface between emotions and biochemical changes. It's the communicator between the body and the mind. Emotions understand images. Emotions also provoke images. And we then have a flood of neurochemical firings and biochemical relationships associated with that.

But I don't think of imagery as a thing to use. I think of it as a thing that simply is. It's the way that we listen to our bodies. It's the way that we listen when we are engaged with other living things. It is just what is.

Imagery is a way of listening and then recommunicating back. We are listening all the time at some level, otherwise we couldn't walk across the room. It's how we know it's time to close a window because we are cold. Because of the constant clatter in our minds and the misinformation that we are taking in, we don't listen adequately and symptoms build. Sometimes we do listen and don't know what to do about it. Then anxiety starts to grow. Or we listen slightly but push it aside so we can continue with our day jobs. That's when the anxiety turns into an ulcer or something else.

To use imagery as a healing device, you should treat it like a ritual, a meditation where you listen with your senses to what is out of harmony in your life, and then with some intention you reframe the image consciously and reconstruct the ill body or the ruptured relationship. Images also usher into consciousness the invisible, unspoken, ineffable worlds of dreams and visions, and the place of spirits and secret workings of soul.

Listening to images requires some quiet. As I said, we are listening all the time at some level, but true listening—where we are functioning in concert with the information that the body-mind gives us—requires a period of quiet. Maybe a daily period of quiet. Maybe a few years of quiet.

Imagery is very important in the menopausal process. I don't think anyone has a clue about the impact menopause really has on the totality of our being. Our culture has tremendously underestimated the process. I simply don't believe women who say "Well, I went right through it and didn't know the difference." Even knowing it is a natural event, that it's the way life is supposed to be, it can still present one of the biggest challenges ever encountered. Physically, there is no way a person can be fully prepared for it.

It's time to rethink, reformat, revision this business of menopause. Estrogen is capable of speaking loudly and it speaks to every single cell in our bodies. It alters every chemical. You flood a body with estrogen or you take estrogen away, and you haven't got the same body. You also don't have the same emotional structure. Our emotional life is informed by that hormone. It bathes and changes every structure in the brain. Period. So when it starts to move out of your body, nothing is the same.

I suspect that you cannot be the same whether estrogen is replaced or not. Your ovaries are your ovaries and your estrogen is your estrogen, and your body has learned how to cycle with it and it does not know how to do that with something else quite so well. Hormone replacement may manage the symptoms, but that, like so many other things done to women's bodies, should be an informed choice. We should be informed of the alternatives and the possible consequences.

What menopause is not, however, is a medical crisis or event, and under no circumstances should it be treated like one. My profession of psychology has labeled the symptoms as depression, hysteria, anxiety, and all sorts of other claptrap that miss the point. It is a rite of passage to be honored and respected and it should not be confused with a disease. I'll say this once, and probably want to say it again in this conversation: We should feel permission to have troublesome symptoms treated medically. This, though, is a whole different ballgame, far different from turning your body over to "medical management." This is saying, "I'm going through this great big change right now and these symptoms (whatever they are) are getting in the way of my life." It's a different image of self.

On the other hand, I heard just as irresponsible a position from a well-known holistic physician in Germany last year. A collective shudder went through the audience of about 600 people (mostly women), when he told us that under no circumstances should anyone receive hormone replacement therapy (HRT). Instead of using HRT, he said, women should try to find out what message was being sent to them through the symptoms. (Spoken like a guy who has not awakened seventy-five times a night covered in sweat.)

But the symptoms are for me a secondary, minor issue. The main issue to deal with is that you are not the same woman. And this is where imagery can help. Many of us have done a real good job of reinterpreting or reimagining some of the symptoms of menopause. For instance, hot flashes can be imaged as a cleansing process. The analogy I prefer is that it is like the refiner's fire, an alchemist's fire. I don't think the heat is an accident. It is a burning away of the dross, leaving only the gold. Even maybe giving an enhancement of immunity, offering protection from infectious disease. When the flush moves in, this image is so much more useful than "Oh, God, I'm suffocating again. Hand me a fan."

Imagery can be used on other symptoms, such as vaginal dryness, which is not uncommon, and is painful enough in some cases to make intercourse most unpleasant. A patient of mine, a young woman who was thrown into early menopause by chemotherapy, decided to try imagery to help with her problem, since the usually recommended creams and lubricants didn't offer that much relief. She told me with some embarrassment that she spent about ten minutes a day—particularly on those days she expected to make love—imagining hummingbirds depositing sweet nectar in her vagina. She said that when she did this, she was moist, and when she didn't, she was back to her thin, dry tissues.

I think the imaging process is a key to moving into the absolute best, most precious time of our lives. We have a choice here. As I said earlier, the old self as we knew her is simply gone after menopause. We can choose to resurrect ourselves out of the ashes, so to speak, as a glorious new bird, or we can hang in there with the aid of modern science and pretend the whole thing isn't happening. Or, we have still another choice. And it is common. We can decide to lump along into old age. You quit your job, move into a smaller house, buy different clothes (bigger, duller, more comfortable), travel a little, learn to play bridge, settle in for the duration. Not too bad. But I don't think this book is for women who want to lump along. This book is not for people who are comfortable with boredom.

HORMONE REPLACEMENT THERAPY

The current emphasis in medical science regarding menopause is on replacing women's natural hormones with a synthetic version in order to avoid certain health problems such as osteoporosis. At best, this solution is fraught with risk and ill side effects. I asked Jeanne why, if it's so important to have the estrogen, scientists aren't trying to find a way women could continue producing their own hormones?

This question takes me aback. I thought, Why in the world would any woman want to keep producing estrogen for the rest of her life?

Would you want a baby? Would you want a three-year-old around ten years from now? I surprised myself with my emotional response to the question. The specter of eternal youth does have a few drawbacks, and this question raises the same issues that HRT raises.

This is what science knows. Women who are obese have circulating estrogen for a long time after their periods stop. But that's not exactly a practical solution, or a healthy one. The conventional scientific wisdom is that you get so many eggs dealt to you, and when they're gone, that's it folks. It's not outside the realm of the possible, I suppose, to graft, plant, or stimulate more eggs indefinitely. On the other hand, it is pretty clear that breast cancer is related to the length of time estrogen has been circulating. Cancer risk would likely increase whether the estrogen was yours or not. So you might have the same drawbacks with hormone replacement therapy, not to mention the possibility of pregnancy in your old age.

The medical dogma regarding the need for HRT is that it primarily prevents osteoporosis and heart attack. What so many women don't know is that an extremely low-fat diet, along with exercise, calcium, and a few supplements, will do the same thing. Without the side effects. So, we're back to where we started—reimagining menopause so that we hold it as the serious challenge it is, and at the same time staying consciously involved in the richness of the experience.

BEING PRESENT FOR THE DARK NIGHT OF THE SOUL

If you look at any dark night of the soul, there is no way to make it pleasant.[2] Any jumping over the abyss, which this is, is very scary.

[2] The "dark night of the soul" is a phrase used by St. John of the Cross to describe the experience of mystics who felt depressed and isolated, even from God, prior to attaining a transcendental state.

I've spent most of my life trying to make people feel better about crisis. You can feel better about it, but I think when you are in it, it is still a very dark night. Knowing that it's part of the refining process, knowing that it may feel like a desert, but a lush one in many ways, might help. But it is not going to make it go away, unless the whole life change is denied completely. But denial does not really make it go away and I think women who do this are missing the opportunity of a lifetime.

If a woman says, "I am simply going to go about my business, get my face lift, get my estrogen replaced, and I'll never know the difference," then she is missing an initiatory rite. Such women will end up in an entirely different place than those who go through the process deliberately. Women have never had the opportunity to keep hormones flowing, they never were able to go to the table to have their faces lifted. It is a new opportunity, one that women have never had in the history of our species. But that fork is choosing not to be present. Not in a wrong way, it's just choosing not to be present.

Now, being present means staying conscious. We all know ways *not* to stay conscious. There are plenty of those. But staying conscious is another matter. I like "mindfulness meditation" because it's teaching me to stay conscious of who I am and how I feel and what kind of response is going on around me.[3] There's a clarity with be-

---

[3] "Practicing mindfulness in Buddhism means to perform consciously all activities including everyday automatic activities such as breathing and walking, and to assume the attitude of pure observation through which clear knowledge, i.e., clearly conscious thinking and acting, is attained. In the practice of perfect mindfulness (Eight-Fold Path) one begins by rendering conscious the individual activities of the body. Then one extends mindfulness to sense data, thinking, and the objects of thinking. The intention of mindfulness practice is to bring the mind under control and to a state of rest. This practice brings insight into the transitory, unsatisfying, and essenceless nature of all existence and is thus the basis for all higher knowledge." From the *Encyclopedia of Eastern Philosophy and Religion* published by Shambala Press, Boston, 1989.

ing present. It is being willing to really taste what is going on in life for you without any anesthesia.

Mindfulness meditation is actually a practice in a number of spiritual traditions. A similar process is also used in stress management programs. Essentially, you let yourself get quiet and attend to whatever comes into your mind. Attention is gentle and detached. You don't get too involved with your thoughts—you just watch what comes up.

Staying present is important in making the menopausal journey. For me, it's important to be there. There are many ways to do it and one of the choices is to press it as far as you can and create as much as you can out of it. I think that is my choice.

USING IMAGERY TO HELP GUIDE

The images you have are there for a reason. What do they tell you? Obviously nature is speaking to you at some cellular level. What is the message from the nature spirit? What is it reflecting for you? Perhaps it's reflecting a bodily change or loss?

You mentioned that when your body was in menopause, you felt like you were dying. You also said your body felt like a lush forest that was turning into a desert. What wonderful imagery, and how much that tells me about your inner life. Why don't we use that as an example of how to engage the imagination in a positive and very large way?

Deserts are really quite beautiful, aren't they? But they do have to grow on you. Eventually you notice you have an unfettered view of the sky, something you never had in the forest or the jungle. The cloud formations, the changing light, the living rocks. And, I don't know about you, but I see spirits out of the corner of my eye in the desert—more than any place else in the world. The beauty there is less organic, more lasting, more skyward. And much more magic. So embracing the image is really about embracing a new form of beauty, and if you respond to it in that manner it will be healing.

One of my students, who is large in size, told me that when menopause started for her, she began to feel lighter and lighter. That in and of itself was a promise to her. She said that for her, from the beginning, it was an unfolding of relief. Her image was not of drying up. It was of becoming lighter and lighter. And, like many menopausal women, she is actually losing quite a bit of weight.

Let me tell you a funny story about my fiftieth birthday, which was the hardest birthday I've ever had. Who in the heck wants to turn fifty? First of all, I am very attached to my femininity and my appearance. I love the deep feminine. So when menopause started, I felt big and fat, just on principle. I have always been a small person and I started gaining weight. I went out the week before my fiftieth birthday and bought $200 worth of bras at a discount store. Can you imagine how many bras that sum buys? I bought a 36C, except I've worn a 34C since I had my children and have never changed. But I went out and bought these huge bras because that was my image of self.

After paying $200, I couldn't throw them away, so I hand-tucked them all. It took me hours of sewing, but they never fit. And they will never fit.

So mine was not an image of lightness. My whole imagery sense was one of darkness, heaviness. If you were entering the desert, I was going underground. I dropped my seeds into the ground and stayed there. One of the ninety-six-year-old woman healers to whom I've gone for advice said that I needed to connect to the oak tree, to connect underground with its roots. So we had a path made down into our property to this 200-year-old oak and I started sleeping under it. When it turned cold, we put a tent down there and I slept in that.

I never articulated this before, but I think what I was doing was gathering the images that were being given, that are generated from soul stuff, and creating ritual from them. Everybody will have their own images. So the process is to let the images inform your meditations or whatever you are doing for yourself.

You need to know that I hadn't had a period from October through February of that year. The first night I slept outside under the oak, I ovulated and my periods started again. Something got resolved when I finally did that. That's why I think there is reason to pay attention to the ebb and flow of life. It's not just hormones.

I've had so many women tell me, "This happened in my life and then my periods stopped forever." For instance, a woman in one of my workshops told me that her periods stopped when her nineteen-year-old son died. Another said her periods stopped when she was thirty-seven, the month her husband confessed to having an affair with his secretary for eight of their ten married years. Both of these women, having suffered a mortal wound to the essence of womanhood, fell down, mourned, got back up on their feet, and back to life. One is a well-published author on women's spirituality, the other engaged her creative force in being a single mom. Only their bodies chose not to reengage in reproductive life.

So menopause appears to be a cultural phenomenon as well as a biological phenomenon. It definitely goes beyond some little clock ticking away in your body.

Of course, the occurrence of these traumatic events may not be cause and effect at all. It may be synchronicity. It may be that these two things are happening together now in one's life. But isn't that part of paying attention and staying present? To watch for these?

Let me describe what happens, using biological terms. There is a biological analog, because biology is just another level of description of what is going on. When chemicals in your body shift there are, first of all, huge emotional changes, and when there are emotions, your chemicals change. For me, menopause was the feeling that something dark had infiltrated my whole body/mind, particularly my brain. It felt like a light went out. And, in fact, biologically, there is a light that goes out when that much hormonal shift is going on. I've seen it before. People with crisis and in trauma, people who have been severely burned or injured, for instance, will often pull the covers over their head. It's not depression. It's called conservation reaction. They don't move. Sometimes the hospital staff get anxious about them and they want to medicate them for depression, but that's not it at all. They are conserving their strength. It's a quiet time of preparation and conservation.

This goes back to my image of being under the ground—protecting, hibernating, waiting, conserving in the darkness for whatever. I've had no need to be under the tree recently. We had reports of a mountain lion in the area and then the tent blew over during the last period of bad weather. So I decided the tree and I had best come to a temporary parting of ways. You see, it's a process. I can't articulate it better than that. But I am no longer underground.

THE DEEP FEMININE

In understanding menopause, it's necessary to look at the deep feminine. The deep feminine is the quintessential feminine. It's the feminine in every sense of the word, not only the cultural concept but also the biological concept of woman. Intuition, giving birth, nurturing, nesting—all the things that we do.

Anthropologists use the word *deep* when referring to universal structures. A deep structure is a universal or an archetypal structure. It's fascinating being in England and in Europe because all of their structures for the feminine are these spiraling things that go down toward the center of the earth. The underworld. Very, very traditional.

And what's down there is life and death. Joseph Campbell said that women always represented life and death and the knowledge of what came up from the ground. He said that people assumed that all life came from the ground because everything they ate came from the ground and all death went in the ground.[4] That made women's power pretty awesome actually, and pretty scary.

One aspect of being underground is that creativity appears to be absolutely paralyzed, when in reality it is being regenerated. You have to come back out before you witness it. In researching people who live by their creative arts, many of them are diagnosed as serious manic-depressives, and many will deliberately invoke depression because they know when they come back out they are massively creative again. So going underground may be a necessary, preparatory stage for more creativity.

When I went back into the ground, it was to see what was down there, to remind myself what was down there. And what was down there was a death. The light is back on now, but had I not lived consciously through the experience, I don't know if I would be the same person now. My consciousness, and consequently my life, would be different.

A HEALING CAME OUT
OF THE JOURNEY

The year I started sleeping outside and trying to find my new life and connect underground with the old tree, I learned how to heal with my hands. Now, that is something I never believed in, but Frank was having a gout attack. We were up in the middle of nowhere and he had horrible pain and we were desperate.

What happened was that I suspended my language, my words, for probably the first time in my entire life. I suspended the language function, and when I did that I could feel what people call "energy."

---

[4]In *The Power of Myth* (Anchor Books) Joseph Campbell says, "Then there is a deeper experience, too, the mystery of the womb and the tomb. When people are buried, it's for rebirth. That's the origin of the burial idea. You put someone back into the womb of mother earth for rebirth. Very early images of the Goddess show her as a mother receiving the soul back again."

Somehow it began speaking to me in images and then I would translate the images with my hands. That's all I can say about it.

I know it wasn't just my imagination and Frank's need to get well. Science has now identified that there's a skeleton on each cell that resonates in response to vibration. It responds to many things, but if you put two cells in a petri dish together, they'll start vibrating at the same rate. So if you have the ability to send a tremendous amount of vibration to your hands, which healers apparently do, you can cause a change in vibration in the other person which seems to facilitate healing.

I don't know whether I could have done that earlier, before I went through all this darkness and connected underground with nature.

RELATIONSHIPS

When the life change happens, at every level most of life changes. All of those people in that human web we've been weaving touch and are touched by this process. How else can it be? Not coincidentally, grown children leave home, others come back (yikes), husbands may pass on or out, or they may have retired and we get to have the pleasure of their company for breakfast, lunch, and dinner. And if we are in close relationship with a mate—man or woman—of our own age, they are going through a similar body/mind/spirit challenge. Count on it. If our chosen one is a lot younger, the issues are different but no less a challenge to our mettle. I suggest we think of menopause not as a personally isolated and isolating phenomenon, but one that is vastly knit into a social and family context.

I believe we women are holding the searchlight over our heads as we all walk this strange new road, asking serious questions not only of menopause but also of aging, and on the structure of relationship.

Aging men are also dealing with something that is big and unknown in terms of the male process during that period. What men have typically done is to try to bolster themselves up with sports cars or new women or any other blessed thing that gives them a testosterone burst, and for good reason because testosterone does go down with age. But men, too, are growing older in the resonant company of their loved ones. There's an interesting study showing that when wives of impotent men are given estrogen, the impotency stops. Is it cause and effect? Or maybe impotent men cause depleted estrogen in their women. Most likely, both are the case. Women living together also pace each other's hormones. Like it or not, we are in this bubbling chemical cauldron together.

It's always easier to talk about the biology than the more fundamental, distinctly human issues and challenges in relationship, such as "where does life derive its meaning and beauty now that we've crossed another threshold together?" I think it might be useful for both parties in a relationship to do some mutual imaging of a new and elected role. I should emphasize "elected." For once in our lives, we can choose without being driven by the so-called biological imperative and the artificial and difficult standards and expectations of being young.

One man friend of mine is living his symbolic process this way. For decades he jokingly referred to himself as a knight in shining armor, in service to his queen. Well, the old knight got wounded. His company downsized, he got fired just before retirement, and the you-know-what hit the fan at home. His queen was no prize either, having ruled too long the queendom by herself while he did the man thing at the office. He now says he is beginning to think of himself as a king instead of a knight. He thinks of himself as a benevolent king, who has the time and patience to reengage in family life.

Have you ever watched a loving couple together? I have. I even had the nerve to follow one elderly couple through the Seattle airport. What a miracle. They were incredibly attractive, in their seventies, and obviously attracted to each other, holding hands, laughing. They had obviously danced and moved in concert with each other for a lifetime. What was their story? What was their image of themselves at the edge of their lives? It is time to start gathering this information, storing it in our communal mind, and living whatever it is for each one of us. Menopause is the time to shift into a new relationship with ourselves and our special loved ones.

FINDING COMMUNITY

It seems to me that as we negotiate the changes we encounter in midlife, the issue of community comes up again and again. Those of us who wish to stay creatively alive are reaching out for one another, and craving the pleasure of having like-minded souls around as we age. I don't know about you, but up until now I was just too busy to even think about community. My community was all over the world. I was all over the world. As gratifying as that peripatetic lifestyle was, I now want to be able to stay a little closer to home and still have the magnificent company to which I have become accustomed.

Having community is also a sense of place, and for me there is an important interactive process with the spirit of the earth that is as necessary as human company. But then I'm not a New Yorker. Maybe city people have different needs.

One of my former students who is now in her late fifties called and said that they had found a nursery on eighty acres south of San Francisco. It has a 100-year-old farmhouse on the property and room for about four couples to both work and live. How delicious for them, I thought, to have an extended family to grow old with. But that lifestyle is not for me. My idea of community for my golden years is one where a weird, wild, irresponsibly dressed old woman who is so engrossed in an idea that she forgets what street she is on and cooks dinner twice in one night won't get arrested for being daffy.

So this is a community dream, and I think it is one much of our generation shares. The question to be puzzled over is whether you are being nourished by the place you live and the company you keep. If so, splendid. If not, there are some exciting choices that you can make in terms of leaving toxic people and places and heading for what makes you feel better.

The business of community is also vital to health. There have been many scientific studies conducted that show the positive impact of social support on health and longevity. And many studies have been done on the elderly. What I like about these studies is the importance of the presence of women. If you are a man and married, you simply live longer and better than single men (not to mention having your socks match up). But if you are a woman, it is not so much the marriage, as having women friends that predicts health and life.

Staying in the Web

I think it needs to be said over and over that menopause is not done in a vacuum. It's not just a woman having a problem. It's experienced in a whole social context. Whether we are in partnership or in friendship or whatever, we are still vibrating each other's microtubules. We affect each other's hormones. Life is a stew.

I have a glimmer of an image and it is one where living is easier than what we are experiencing and where there is more human contact, where the pressures to stay mentally engaged, or at least creatively engaged, are there.

Some of the most interesting research is being done on people who are a hundred years or older. The researchers have isolated four common characteristics. One characteristic is that these people are engaged in something, that they are passionate about something. Another is optimism. Another is that their caloric intake is higher and they are physically quite active. And last, they have learned ways to deal with their significant losses.

In my research for the book *Uncommon Bonds* I've been looking at historical people to whom everyone felt a special kinship. For instance, consider the women who had the eighteenth-century poets and philosophers in Europe at their feet. There is something special about those people. Some of these women were old and everyone said they were homely, there was never any question about it, and yet their list of lovers included every vital, interesting, important man in Europe and the United States. One of the women, I don't even remember her name (but Voltaire and others loved her deeply), was described in her sixties and seventies as still having men falling down around her. She was the *only* love of several of these men and they all said it was because she was so nice. So *nice*.

Obviously, I was curious about this. These women kept people in the web, so to speak. They stayed connected. One of the things often said about these people who continue to hold the interest of others all their lives is that they smell so good. There is something called the odor of sanctity. When talking about the saints, some people said you could walk into a room where they were and smell an odor of violets or other flowers. Then I read that in the menopause years you start smelling different because many of the wonderful lusty molecules shift. So maybe smell becomes a different sort of pleasure. Maybe the new smells set off all sorts of different bells. But this is yet another thing that keeps people in the web together. It's that some senses are provoked. And you see, none of these things have to do with youth or attractiveness.

However, our culture is not training women to be nice and we are not training women to listen and we are not training women to be keepers of the web. We are training women to break things instead of teaching them to keep weaving. To be a weaver doesn't mean you can't be bitchy, because some of the nicest women I know have a real edge to them when they are protecting what they need to protect. Being a weaver means you keep mending the web.

You just don't see too many holy women in our society. And that's the problem. We need to rethink what is truly holy and we need to make this part of culture, part of what we women become.

THE HERO'S JOURNEY IS INCOMPLETE

I have to tell you that, for women, I challenge the monomyth of Campbell. I have had a hero's journey in my life. I have embraced the hero's path—seeking bliss, conquering demons, striving for a higher cause, emerging through crisis into a state of majestic triumph, and attempting to leave an indelible mark on the cultural landscape. But if I were to speak honestly, it was just a hobby, a pastime. The real life that I have lived is one of communion, of nurturing, and of tending relationships.

I no longer believe the full journey for women is an ascendance process. I think it is lateral and not hierarchical. The analogy that is used so often is one of a web. What women continue to do is to shake the web. We make more and more filaments across and through the web with our children, with our love relationships, with our students and our patients, always bringing them into some kind of unitive webness.

Another analogy that comes to mind are the myths of the twenty-four-hour weavers who are always reweaving their fabrics.[5] Bringing in lost pieces. Mending the tears. Now in this journey, you are not going anywhere. You are not going out. And that is very different from the hero's journey.

[5] The three weavers appear in fairy tales from many cultures. Best known in our society is the story from the Grimm collection known as "The Three Spinners," which he believed to be a "broken" version of the "Three Spinning Fates" in European mythology. From the *Encyclopedia of Eastern Philosophy and Religion*.

One of the most intriguing bits of information, which comes from Plato and some of the philosophers of the past century and which is currently being reaffirmed by Stan Grof in some of his altered state work, is that the myth is alive. Even Carl Jung, as he grew very old and very wise, felt that the myth was ongoing. In fact, Jung said that the hardest thing that he had to deal with intellectually was that those mythic realities have a life of their own. He felt that in certain circumstances, we have access to other realities either with the dream life or with altered states and that in those realities, the mythical stories, the deep structure stories, are being played out.

Some believe these stories predate humanity, that they are there to assist in the evolution of consciousness, to teach us our own story, and how to fully live our lives. Therefore, there is great value in seeking these landscapes.

Now let me take this one outrageous step farther. I do not believe a satisfactory landscape has yet been devised in this reality or the mythic reality that has the elements we women who are aging seek. It is now up to us fragile, mortal creatures to architect and midwife another myth. We have to plant trees, envision people, design relationships and communities. And in this new land we will find adventure and passion and creativity and challenge and beauty and power.

WOMEN'S POWER

Early in our relationship, Jeanne sent me part of a manuscript she was writing. She captured my attention in the first few paragraphs when she wrote: "Many women, like me, cannot name their spiritual tradition. My own restless spiritual life is mirrored by the difficult and majestic landscape, by fermenting winds and weather, by waves crashing on the dangerous rocks below. My faceless divinity has no name and the prayers have no special language. I must gather strength and wisdom from process rather than form—from listening, from peering through layers of veils that separate the worlds, and from falling into the abyss and surrendering to the possibility that I might not survive the fall."

Jeanne's words articulated what I had felt for years. I have no church, no group, no one single practice, no name for my god and no name for what I do. Although I've practiced meditation, I have never been able to embrace it as an exclusive *practice because meditation has never satisfied my deep need to create. As a discipline, it teaches you to exist in a state of what I call "no create." The is-ness and now-ness and liberation of mindful observation and "no create" is a very wonderful place. But there is something lacking in it for the part of me that is the deep feminine creative force. I always end up feeling disturbed, as if I am only seeing part of what there is to be seen.*

I have never been able to reconcile this split, and I know that neither have many of my friends, so I asked Jeanne to tell of her experience.

The question is, what is women's practice? I think it's life. I think it's creation. Many people believe that you can't really be enlightened until you follow the meditative path, but that's more old dogma that doesn't really fit women's experience.

What you are saying is that you don't want to insulate yourself against the world. You want to be part of the world. You want to shake the web. And you don't do that in meditative practice. I know the stuff about "if you could change yourself and give unconditional love, you could change the world." No doubt this is subtle truth. And the good aspect of meditation is that you get into the silence and you do connect with that unconditional love. But then I say, now that I'm connected, what's the next step? And it's not there.

I think our spiritual discipline is life. When I talk to my women friends about this, they tell me the same is true for them. Their religion gives them grounding of sorts, but they have to work through and into the everyday things to find the deepest truths.

The spirituality in everyday life is the wheel of Samsara, in the Buddhist tradition.[6] Our wheels are paced by the moon cycles, and ebb and flow of ocean tides, and brought from youth to old age by the unspoken tryst with nature. In primitive cultures, the feminine cycles were believed to be participatory in keeping the earth on its axis and the sun in the sky. So not only did women draw energy from the earth, but by engagement with the life cycle we returned energy as well.

This may be a better view. When we grow through the stages of our own unfolding, we eventually find ourselves in uncomfortable straight-backed chairs of the public sphere. It is no longer enough to send love and light to the world through prayer and deep meditative practice, for we are heralds of the fate of those we love. We have to take our responsibility as the holders of traditions and the keepers of the community in a most serious vein. It is not enough to awaken self, find community, and share the sacrament with like-minded people in order to fulfill our contracts. The world itself needs restructuring.

[6] Samsara is the cycle of birth, death, and rebirth to which every human being is subject so long as we live in ignorance and do not know our identity with Brahma. Samsara is the cycle of existences, a succession of rebirth that a being goes through within various modes of existence, until it has attained liberation and entered nirvana. From the *Encyclopedia of Eastern Philosophy and Religion*.

PART SEVEN

Remembering

and the Ways

of Knowing

I HAVE ALWAYS BEEN FASCINATED with the concept of intuition, the rather magical ability Carl Jung described as "seeing around corners." Intuition is an elusive talent and often defined by what it is not. It is "the act or faculty of knowing without the use of rational process."[1] It is seeing without using your eyes, hearing without using your ears, and knowing without being told. The Latin origins of the word *intuit* are *in*, meaning "in" and *tueri*, meaning "to look at." The concept of "to look at in" tells us much about intuition.

For many reasons, I have long believed that developing and using intuition is a reasonable idea. For instance, the future may bring unpleasant surprises, some of which might be avoided, contained, or at least met with preparation if you employ the intuitive sense. People have agendas and don't always tell the truth. It is always useful to know when this is happening. We are constantly bombarded with data, all of which require sifting, sorting, judging, filing. Intuition can help us choose which facts we need to pay attention to when. Furthermore, much of the information available to us lies in the unconscious or unseen realm. Intellectually, rationally, we are barely cognizant of it and rarely access it, even though it holds the deepest, most potent secrets of our lives. Often, the intuitive can open this door.

---

[1] *Webster's II New Riverside University Dictionary,* Houghton Mifflin Company, Boston, 1984.

For these reasons I have sought means to increase my own understanding and use of intuition. My direct experience with it is varied and probably similar to that of most people reading this book. Sometimes I know things that by any reasonable explanation I shouldn't know. For instance, I remember being at work one day and suddenly getting the idea that my husband David was out at sea. When I arrived home that evening I discovered the hunch was correct. He had, in fact, gone sailing with a client.

Sometimes when a person is speaking to me, I will receive an idea about them. Ten minutes, two days, or two years later, they, or someone else, may tell me the same exact information. For example, years ago there was a certain person at my office with whom I had a difficult time communicating. One night I had a dream about his mother. In the dream this woman was quite mean to her child and so the child withdrew and became devious. The very next day, this same person mentioned that he'd had a difficult relationship with his mother.

Not all of my intuitions are verified in such a neat and timely manner, but I've learned to trust the information I receive in this way, whether it is confirmed or not.

Another type of intuitiveness I experience is being allowed a glimpse into the future. When this happens, the future appears before me in a vision so clear and precise that I dare say I see it with my eyes. The vision doesn't last as something I can see, but integrates itself into my body instead. I'm left not with facts or an idea I can articulate but with a deep cellular knowing. My mind/body then becomes an effective "early warning detection system," steering me along the future's path with physiological sensations.

One of the best examples of this, I think, is how I found my current job. I saw a fleeting vision of it, very quick, and understood that it was good. Then, about five weeks later, while reading the want ads in the Sunday edition of the *San Diego Union*, I was filled with a strong feeling of recognition and an even stronger tingling in my chest and arms. The overwhelming sense was that this was my future's path, my destiny. My body wanted to go. The company was located fifty miles up the coast, and it wasn't exactly what I thought I had in mind, but I followed my intuition and applied anyway. Two months later I was hired. Four and a half years later, I'm still there and still enjoying the wonderful opportunities that it provides.

Intuition plays a big role in my life, not only because I try to nurture that aspect of self but also because I am surrounded by people who live intuitively. One day back in 1989, when David and I were still dating, we were driving around Central City, Colorado. He was telling me about an idea he had for a wind-up flashlight that didn't need batteries. All of a sudden he stopped the car. "Let's go in that antiques store," he said, pointing to a place he was seeing for the first time in his life. We parked and went inside. David walked to the back of the store and looked into a crowded glass case, full of trinkets and bottles and gadgets. There at the very back of the case was an antique flashlight, designed on the very same energy principles he had been describing to me.

One morning as I was getting ready to go to work, my two-and-a-half-year-old son said to me, "Watch out for the car, Mom." I paid heed to his little voice. Sure enough, three minutes later as I was pulling out into the alley behind our house, a white car came speeding down the lane, missing me by inches.

It seems to me that we shouldn't ignore or deny something so evident and so present and so helpful in our lives. I know that intuition is often smirked at in scientific circles and frowned upon in religious halls, but it is part of the human experience. It is also not new to the twentieth century. It has been used, studied, talked about, and pursued since man first walked the earth.

There is a wonderful book titled *The World Atlas of Divination* that traces the use of divination, including intuition, from man's earliest beginnings.[2] Different cultures have developed different methods of accessing intuitive powers, but knowledge about and reliance on the unseen realms for aiding survival in this world is a common thread that weaves its way through humankind's history.

In this book, Peter Taylor writes eloquently of a commonly held theory about why intuition is possible and how it works. Talking about the early European healers, Taylor explains that the runes were used as gateways. "This is neither going into the past nor into the future; it is entering into that condition where everything actually is, the eternal present moment."[3]

Please don't confuse the caring people who use tools such as tarot, bones, runes, the *I Ching,* astrology, and geomancy to deepen their relationship with life, with those who play parlor games and take your money to predict when you might next fall in love and with whom. These systems of divination are more than simply ways of knowing. They are also used, and perhaps *primarily* used, as a means for finding our correct relationship with all that is and understanding our universe. They are tools for growth and survival. Michael Harner, in *The Way of the Shaman,* talks about the "big dream," explaining that they are messages from the spirit world about future events and how they help us be prepared.[4] In his book, *The Tarot,* Alfred Douglas explains that the tarot speaks to us through "the language of the unconscious, and when approached in the right manner it may open doors into the hidden reaches of the soul."[5] He says that the tarot images stimulate one's own intu-

---

[2] Matthews, John, ed. *The World Atlas of Divination,* Bulfinch Press, Little, Brown and Company, Boston, 1992.

[3] Taylor, Peter. "The Message of The Runes," chapter four of *The World Atlas of Divination,* page 44.

[4] Harner, Michael. *The Way of the Shaman,* HarperCollins, San Francisco, 1990, pages 99–101.

[5] Douglas, Alfred. *The Tarot,* Penguin Books, New York, 1972, pages 43, 44.

itive processes that then lead to understandings "outside the scope of the intellect." In his translation of the Chinese *Book of Changes*, a text some 3,000 years old, Richard Wilhelm refers to the *I Ching* as both the "book of oracles" and "the book of wisdom." Wilhelm wrote, "In discerning with its help the seeds of things to come, we learn to foresee the future as well as understand the past."[6]

For many years, when I felt occluded or confused, I would consult the *I Ching* or my tarot cards. Both helped me see the events of my life in a broader context. Then in 1992, while in Canada for Christmas, David's oldest sister gave me a book with an accompanying deck of cards. I had an immediate sense that it was, for me, a magic book. It was called *Medicine Cards,*™ and was written by Jamie Sams and David Carson.

The book and cards compose a system of divination to help people find their own connections to the universe and understand their relationships within those connections. And, as Jamie Sams wrote, "We are in an age that has severed itself from nature and magic. The Medicine Cards are a method for remedying that dissociation."[7] The book was compiled from the teachings of the Choctaw, Lakota, Seneca, Aztec, Yaqui, Cheyenne, Cherokee, Iroquois, and Mayan traditions. *Medicine Cards* spoke to me in a very gentle but very real and powerful way. The best explanation I can give is to quote part of a meditation written by Sams for the fourth day of the second moon in her book *Earth Medicine*.

THE DANCE OF REMEMBERING

"What is the Remembering, Grandmother?" the young woman asked. And the Wise One replied, "The Remem-

---

[6] Wilhelm, Richard, trans. *The I Ching or Book of Changes,* third edition, Princeton University Press, 1950.

[7] Sams, Jamie, and David Carson. *Medicine Cards,* Bear & Company, Santa Fe, 1988, page 17.

bering is many things, because it is a gradual unfoldment of the Spiritual Essence. The Remembering takes form when human beings come fully alert, aware of all that has come before, their rightful place in Creation, and choice of paths the Great Mystery gave them. Then the Ancestor Spirits tell the awakened humans how to accomplish their tasks in life through the use of their own good Medicine."[8]

Since that Christmas, I have used the Medicine Cards to access my intuition or see an event in context or guide me in problem solving. They have served me well, and after I always sent a silent intent of thanks to the authors for creating this beautiful tool, which is why, when a friend asked if I'd like to meet Jamie Sams and interview her, I was delighted. This wise woman was already part of my life and now she would be part of my book.

Jamie Sams lives in the foothills outside Santa Fe, New Mexico, in a warm and enchanting adobe house. I interviewed her in the spring, the season of new beginnings and new life and new awarenesses.

Jamie is part Cherokee, part Seneca, and part French. Her life is as varied as her ethnicity. She is a midwife who has successfully delivered over 150 babies, an award-winning chef, an author, a songwriter, and a poet. At one point in her life she owned a successful catering company in Hollywood. At another point she made and sold turquoise jewelry on the streets. Now she enjoys the life of an author and teacher.

Destiny also handed her physical challenges. While living and studying with three of her Native elders in Mexico, Jamie fell through a roof and broke her back. She had a hysterectomy at age twenty-eight, and suffered from chronic fatigue syndrome and undulant fever in her thirties. Today, she is in good health. She's a

[8] Sams, Jamie. *Earth Medicine*, HarperCollins, San Francisco, 1994, page 34.

healer and mentor and founder of the Native American Tribal Traditions Trust, an organization that provides books and scholarship
money to Native Americans, and access to traditional native medicine through the "elders travel funds."

Jamie brings two unique gifts to this book. First is her understanding of creation and of the creative process. This is vital information for menopausal women. As we enter our most powerful
years, the time in our lives when we can contribute *with wisdom* to
our cultures, we need to know of how to manifest our dreams. Her
second gift is the intuitive Medicine Card reading she performed
for menopausal women in America. She has provided us with a
connection to the unseen realm and offered us a bridge to ourselves, a path on which we can make a successful journey. In short,
Jamie's reading holds the keys for our Remembering.

Jamie Sams

CREATION

Women give birth to their dreams through their womb. People think it's through the heart or mind or something else, but it's not. It's through the womb space. The connection to your gifts, your talents, your abilities, and your creativity all comes from the womb. And even if you are like me and your womb has been removed, your *womb space* is still intact.

Sky

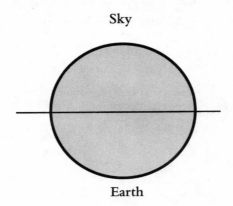

Earth

Put a circle in front of you. From east to west there is a horizon line. Everything on the bottom of the circle is earth and everything on the top of the circle is sky. When we look at how we create things as human beings, the very first step of any creation is desire. You have to want to create it. You have to have that desire. Having these emotions intact is ultimately important because desire comes from passion and passion comes from the ovaries.

People talk about men who have cojones and women who

have chutzpah. All that is is passion for life and it comes from the genitals, from the earth.

So the first step of creation is desire. Now, your heart and your mind are intertwined, and your mind can thwart your heart's desire. That happens with everyone a million times in their lives. In *Earth Medicine,* I said that "human desire is the active ingredient that continues to create the self, unless thwarted by lack of imagination. Weaves the Web, the Clan Mother of the Tenth Moon Cycle, reminds us not to tangle our creativity with limiting lies that alter our potential for living." But you can't always depend on the heart, so you have to depend on the womb.

Let's go back to the circle. Let's say you have this wonderful idea and there it is in the thought universe. It's not in form yet; it's still an idea of the sky, of the air, of the spirit world. How do you make that idea manifest in physical reality? You bring it down from the sky into the earth.

Most women are never taught that vaginal exercises are actually grounding. It brings the Earth Mother's energy into your body. It activates your womb and activates your passion. And that passion does not have to be used for sexuality. It can be used for creativity. So you need to take your idea and bring it down into your body. In the Bible, in the Christian and Judeo traditions, the Old Testament says, "Gird your loins with power." In the Chinese Taoist tradition, there is a power stance for the martial arts, because the body's center of gravity is in the hips, along a line that goes directly across the top of the ovaries.

So if you want to bring the dream into being, you use this beautiful body that you have been given to walk it, to take action, to make it happen. But you have to ask for something that most people who are on a spiritual path have not recognized. They go to their spirit guides or to Jesus or Buddha or Krishna or Mohammad, and make their prayers. People do this all over the world, in every different religion. But they forget that all that beautiful spirituality is still in heaven, the spirit world, the thought universe. It is not here. And until they ask the Earth Mother's blessing, it cannot manifest on this physical plane.

So people cut the circle in half on the horizon, judging that the sky and ideas and spirituality are far more superior than the physical. In that way, they have created the abyss that separates them from the beauty of their own humanity.

The Earth Mother is a living, breathing entity. She does not separate the energy of the sky from the things of physicality.

THE GRANDMOTHER LODGE

It's time for women to see that in many other cultures, every wrinkle on your face is a mark of wisdom. To move into the wisdom lodge is an incredible thing. But if you have not nurtured the wisdom and if you have not honored the experiences along the way, then the last thing that women want to see is wrinkles on their face and gray in their hair.

The wisdom lodge or Grandmother lodge was originally a place for older women to counsel the younger women who were going from adolescence through puberty into womanhood. It was a place for young mothers to leave their children while they went to the Moon lodge. The grandmothers would nurture and pamper the children and teach them things and tell them stories.

I come from two matrilineal societies—the Seneca and Cherokee. In both these traditions, the women own the land and all the possessions of the house. If the men wanted to go to war, the elder women's lodge, which was the Grandmother lodge, would be the ones to say yea or nay, because they were going to be the ones that would have to raise the children alone if the men were killed.

So decisions were made from a place of wisdom inside the

Grandmother lodge. The little girls who had just become women, the young married women, and the women who were coming upon middle age, would all sit and listen to the elder women in the Grandmother lodge. Women would learn how to think, how to be industrious, how to be problem solvers and peace keepers and good mothers. They would learn how to nurture children and how to look at each child individually to discover what his or her gifts and talents were and how to support that. And the wise women would learn to take a child to the person in the tribe who had that same gift or talent, to make sure that the child would develop his or her full potential.

As living extensions of the Earth Mother, the women understood the difference between male and female rain, and how to plant things that were interdependent in mounds instead of in long crop rows like they do now. Squash, beans, and corn would be planted together in the same mound. The cornstalk becomes the poles that the beans grow up and the leaves from the beans and corn make shade for the squash as it grows down the mound. These plants were called the three sacred sisters. The women understood that everything was interrelated.

The Grandmother lodge was a place for woman elders to go if they were beyond their bleeding years and needed to come together for a time of quiet. They would go to the Grandmother lodge and discuss how they could help tribal members who were off balance. Anything they chose to do was honored as wisdom. Everything was shared.

A person's value to the tribe was always determined by the honesty, generosity, and willingness to pitch in long before being asked. That willingness is what developed gifts, talents, and abilities within women. They saw themselves as contributors and creatresses.

We are the nesters. We are the nurturers. Anything that helps bring harmony into the home is a good idea.

THE NOW

In the Seneca tradition, there are seven sacred directions: East, South, West, North, Above, Below, and *Within*. In the Cherokee tradition there are seven sacred directions: East, South, West, North, Above, Below, and *Now*. So Within and Now are the same direction. While I was back on our reservation in North Carolina, the ancestors came to me and told me about the seventh direction, the Now. I want to read what I wrote to you, because I feel it pertains to women who are going through change. You have to look at what is happening to you, why it is happening, what the opportunity is, how you can get through it and move on to your next spoke on the wheel, your next level of the dance, your next lessons in life, and reclaim the joy. So this is it:

"From our most profound pain and from our deepest sadness, grow the seeds of our concern, human compassion and caring. The gift of the Now is in feeling all that our sensitivity can embrace. That is why the gift of the Now is called *the Present*.

"To embrace the healing that springs from that sensitivity is an act of courage. Being fully in the Now releases the pain so that we become authentically free."

That is what the passage into wisdom is about and it can take your entire life to be able to embrace all of your sensitivity and all of your feelings, which frees the will, because the will is the emotional body. When you let go of the past and drop your fear of the future, you are fully in the Now, and all seven directions are in balance.

EARTH MEDICINE

My books are medicine, but nothing that I have ever written in any book is privileged or secret information belonging to a specific tribe or medicine lodge. I don't believe that type of information should go out to the public. What I have written about is the medicine of the earth, and that belongs to all five races. I do not believe that the Earth Mother would want any person, any beautiful human being, to be denied the understanding of the planet that we live on and all living things and how we are interdependent and how we are here to love and learn and grow together. There is a lot of "secret information" that has been passed down to me that I would never reveal because it doesn't apply. Unless a person is born into a certain tradition, it's not going to help. But I do believe that the Earth Mother wants the medicine of the earth to be understood—the language of the trees, the language of the animals, the language of the stones, the healing plants, the way that we can show respect. All I am doing is offering an option.

I wrote a book with my grandmother called *Other Council Fires Were Here Before Ours.* According to our Seneca legends, the first race on our planet was the black race. They were the seekers of truth who were unafraid of going into the darkness of the unknown and bringing back the truth. The brown race was next. They were the keepers of women's medicine, the family unit, the connection to the earth, and agriculture and things that grow. The next race was the yellow race, and they were the keepers of the wisdom of the ancestors and unconditional love. The red race were the keepers of the earth medicine, the language of the trees, the stones, the plants, the interrelatedness of spiritual and physical on the earth plane. And the white race, which was the last race to come to this planet, were given the gifts of magnetism, charisma, and proper use of authority.

I am half white, so I honor both my white side and my red side. I understand that there has to be a balance. You can draw people to you. You can be charismatic and you can learn how to magnetize to you what you need, but when it comes to the proper use of authority, any manipulation or control is an abuse of power that has perpetuated the separation on this planet for the past 60,000 years.

As the Fifth World of Illumination and Peace comes in, all of the five races are going to see a major shift. We are all becoming a potpourri of various genetic blood types and it is important for everyone to understand the balance in that. Instead of saying that this lesson is strictly for the red race or the brown race, all of the lessons of every race apply to everyone. The time for hierarchy is over. Each man, woman, and child on this planet is a medicine person, no matter what race they come from, and all human beings have the mission of healing themselves.

CULTIVATING THE SACRED

My advice to menopausal women is to honor their time. Either during the new moon or the full moon, they should retreat somewhere for three days of total silence. No radios. No recorded music. No telephones. Go somewhere that is safe, once a month, every single month without fail. And that means without other women. You are by yourself.

Many people are scared to death of doing something like this. Even if they rented a cabin and knew that they were perfectly safe, instead of going out and walking in nature where it is wonderful, they would sit inside the cabin with the curtains drawn and be fidgeting or worrying, because they have never felt comfortable with themselves. Once again we are back to vanity. If you see yourself as an object for someone else rather than a person belonging to yourself with your own gifts, talents, and abilities, you don't feel very comfortable being alone.

Everything happens in the silence and nothing can happen in that silence. Even if a person just notices how uncomfortable they are and starts writing down all their feelings, they'll start understanding where some of their confusion comes from. Many women who go on healing quests will sit there for the entire three days feeling frustrated because nothing is happening. What "happens" depends on your patterns and defense mechanisms. You can have expectations, you can project into the future, you can get caught in the past. But if you are in the Now, in the moment, just observing the beauty around, that should be enough because you are not busy doing or thinking or having to have. You are simply being.

The moment you can simply be means you are at peace with yourself. And that's the goal, don't you think?

THE READING

At this point in our conversation, I asked Jamie if she would do a reading for the menopausal women of America. She graciously agreed. She used both her Medicine Cards and Sacred Path Cards. The cards she chose, placed in the teepee spread, are depicted below. Her interpretation follows.

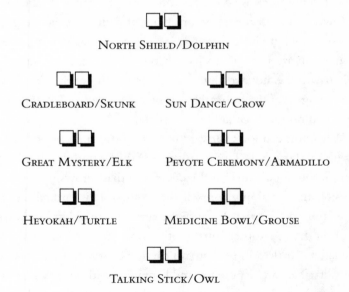

NORTH SHIELD/DOLPHIN

CRADLEBOARD/SKUNK   SUN DANCE/CROW

GREAT MYSTERY/ELK   PEYOTE CEREMONY/ARMADILLO

HEYOKAH/TURTLE   MEDICINE BOWL/GROUSE

TALKING STICK/OWL

This is the teepee spread. I'm going to tell you the position of each one of the cards and how the Sacred Path Cards and Medicine Cards work together. I asked the Earth Mother to bring forth the cards that would give the general, overall holographic archetype women need to know as they make the menopausal rite of passage into the Wise Woman years.

This first position is the past. This represents what is passing away. The Medicine Bowl is the womb and everything comes from the womb. The Grouse is synchronicity. It is cycles. So the cycles of healing and cleansing that came with the bleeding years are what is passing away. That type of synchroneity and the healing that comes with filling the womb with babies is what women are putting behind them.

The next set of cards is the door of the teepee or the present. This is the main lesson for everyone who is going through menopause. The cards are the Talking Stick with Owl. So it's giving yourself as many viewpoints and options as are possible on all levels. Talking Stick is saying no tunnel vision. Since it came with the Owl, it's not deceiving yourself about gaining some weight or getting wrinkled and growing gray. The idea that you are useless because you are not able to have babies anymore, that as an older woman you are not worthy, is a deception. It is what keeps you from seeing all of the doors that are being opened and all the viewpoints and options that are being offered.

What you can look forward to during this time period is Turtle with the Heyokah. This means seeing things with humor. Laugh about it. Don't get stuck in the deception that throws you into the opposite, into devaluing yourself as a woman. This card talks of our connection to the earth, because the turtle is the oldest living symbol of the Earth Mother. Turtle is the most fertile of all animals on this planet. Turtle tells us that you can look forward to a new kind of fertility that can be pure joy and happiness without having to experience the roller coaster effect of PMS and cramps and all the things that we have gone through as women.

The structure that women need at this time is the Peyote Ceremony Card with Armadillo, which means developing new abilities and giving yourself healthy boundaries. In other words, I am not a doormat. This is a time for me. I am willing to accept this and I am not willing to accept that. And developing new gifts, talents, and abilities that allow you to go beyond the former limitations that were created during the childbearing and child-rearing years.

The internal strength or the medicine that women can call on is their connection to the Great Mystery. All life force flows through everything. There is spirit, there is joy, there is connectedness from the original source, and when you turn and look for it within, then you see it within and you start demonstrating that same wisdom, and you become that same unconditional loving attitude. The Great Mystery card came with Elk, which is about stamina, persistence, and health. This is saying the spiritual source is inside you. You can discover all kinds of wonderful things inside you when you discover your spirituality, but balance it with keeping your body strong. Use the persistence and the stamina part of your being to become more physical. Walk in nature. Do things that are going to make all of your organs and all of your body parts strong. Focus on physical health and activity as well as your spiritual side. See them in balance. In other words, bring the heaven into the physical form and walk it. That is the medicine of the wisdom years.

Now, these next two cards are the blessings that are being given even if you have not asked for them. So when you are going through the rite of passage of menopause, you are being given these blessings.

The Sun Dance card with Crow. Crow represents Divine law. The medicine story of Crow is that it pecked at its own shadow until it woke up and ate Crow. So that's self-criticism, self-hatred, self-revilement, low self-worth, and low self-esteem. If you look at the ability to let go of criticizing self, that is the blessing that you are being offered if you fully embrace the wisdom years. You no longer have to constantly peck, peck, peck at what's wrong with you. You need to use Divine law to shift that into looking at what is right with you. It came with the Sun Dance card, which is all about self-sacrifice, so this is saying that women who have spent their lives raising families, taking care of husbands, trying to keep a career going, contributing to everybody else, the only thing that they are being asked to sacrifice now is the limitation and hesitation of being okay with themselves, of loving themselves, and no longer pecking at what is wrong but looking at what is right.

The unexpected challenge of the menopausal years is Skunk. Skunk teaches you to draw to you what you want and deflect what you don't want. Skunk and Cradleboard came together. So it's magnetizing to you what you need and want, and pushing away what you don't want. It's about making those choices simply by how you hold yourself and how you honor the wisdom that you carry. You can draw to you what you truly need and the rest will go away.

Now, we can ask, why is it an unexpected challenge? Because when you get this magnetism going and you are drawing to you what you want and the things that you don't want are simply falling away, how are you going to respond? How are you going to be responsible for suddenly looking at yourself in a different way? You are owning the wisdom that you carry and suddenly what is being drawn to you are younger women, who are asking, "How did you do that?" Suddenly you are in a position where you realize that you have learned a few things in your life and it's time for you to pass those on. How are you going to respond to them? Are you going to take responsibility for those things or are you going to say, "You ought to talk to someone else. I don't know that." So the unexpected challenge for a woman who is moving into her Wise Woman years is to own and share her wisdom and intuition lovingly and willingly with confidence.

The ultimate outcome is, of course, the North Shield, being grateful for the wisdom that you carry. The Dolphin is taking the life manna or the energy that is being funded to you from the earth, from the Creator, and funneling it with gratitude in a circular motion where it doesn't go out and not return, but is moving through you so that you feel the passion and the fire of the earth moving up the back of your body, then changing, going down the front of your body, as water into the core of the earth. You are the circle. You are the living extension of the life force that is the Earth Mother. You are a woman.

Many people have heard that as one door shuts another one always opens. What I would like women who are going into their menopause years to know that it's not just one door shutting and one door opening. If they can see themselves in the center of a circle and recognize that they used to bleed thirteen times a year and that there are thirteen moons a year, they, being in the center of the circle, are being given the opportunity to become their vision, whatever their vision is. And all that needs to happen to become your potential is to feel the true desire and to explore all the doors that are around the circle. Menopause is a time of exploration. It is a time of joyous completion, a time of endings and beginnings, and the transmutation of old belief systems and things that don't apply and a welcoming of the new. It is about healing and becoming whole.

INTUITION

Becoming whole is a skill that, like everything in life, we need to practice. Intuition plays a very big role in becoming whole because intuition teaches us how to trust ourselves and our inner knowing. Every person carries the ability to tap the wisdom of all human beings who have come before us in our individual family trees. The memory of our ancestors is carried in the DNA of the blood, but in Native American traditions, we are not so scientific. We were taught that the blood is the key because it is one of the five water elements in the body, and water or feelings is the source of intuition. Blood flows through the generations carrying physical and spiritual characteristics and the Remembering.

The Remembering is the wholeness we find through using our intuition. Through learning to trust our feelings, we can access what feels right and good, our compassion for others, our sense of truth, our place in the scheme of the universe, what we can contribute, and when we need to advance or retreat in a situation. Intuition comes forth in a more clear and precise way when we are not controlled by our hormones or physical disease. With the natural lessening of hormone production, women begin to use the energy in the womb space for self-development and the Remembering, learning to trust the intuition that comes forth. Developing those skills is an ultimate rite of passage that allows a woman to embrace her potential.

During our bleeding years, we cleanse the womb of all physical buildup of the fertility cycle and the emotional buildup of passions, dreams, intuition, and desires that we carry for ourselves and our families. When, as women, we carry the emotions or fears and pains of others empathically, along with our own judgments and fears, we can experience pain and emotional upset. These symptoms almost always appear when we carry judgments about our bodies, our moon cycles, our sexuality, or our reproductive organs.

Sexual or procreative energy is creative energy that can be used in a multitude of ways. By allowing the energy in the womb space to be transmuted from the physical and used for inspiration, creativity, and intuition, the Wise Woman issues forth, being born from our own wombs to take her place as the women we have the potential to remember and to become. Just as it takes nine months to gestate and birth a baby, the birth we give to our potential selves can take many years because we are continually becoming our highest potential. When we embrace our feelings, we commit to our intuition, which becomes the guide for our evolvement. This cycle is another kind of fertility cycle that teaches us gratitude for the wisdom we carry and for that which we are becoming.

THANK YOU FOR BEING

In the Seneca tradition, the traditional greeting is "Thank you for being." When you come to that place of wisdom, the ultimate joy is in being able to look at another person and say "thank you for being," and meaning it, no matter what they are being at any given moment in time, and not having any judgment and then using that same ability as you turn and face the center of the circle and yourself within.

Thank yourself for being and thank yourself for becoming your vision, your potential. And then be willing to share that unconditional love of self with everyone.

PART EIGHT

Recovering the Old, Creating the New

Our deepest fear is not that we are inadequate.
Our deepest fear is that we are powerful beyond measure.
It is our Light, not our darkness, that most frightens us.
We ask ourselves, who am I to be brilliant, gorgeous, talented, fabulous?
Actually, who are you NOT to be?
You are a child of God. Your playing small does not serve the world.
There is nothing enlightened about shrinking so that other people won't
*   feel insecure around you.*
We were born to manifest the glory of God that is within us.
It is not just in some of us; it is in everyone.
And as we let our own Light shine, we unconsciously give other people
*   permission to do the same.*
As we are liberated from our own fear, our presence automatically liberates
*   others.*

—Marianne Williamson, 1992
A Return to Love

The plum tree in my backyard began its life many years ago. It started as a small seed. As it grew, it matured from seed to sapling to tree. These days, my young son loves to pick its fruit and eat the sweet plums.

In this same way, my interest in mystical practices was born at a very early age. First there was a seed, a thought, a single idea. I was seven or eight when I learned about the Catholic saints in Sunday school. The stories of their lives were captivating, full of mystery, adventure, and extraordinary deeds. My imagination was engaged. My soul was touched.

The nuns explained how St. Bernadette, an ignorant French peasant girl, saw the Virgin Mary at age fourteen. Her visions were so powerful, so real, they said, that a shrine was built to Mary in Lourdes, France. We next studied St. Joan of Arc. I learned that, compelled by visions, this magnificent lady rescued the city of Orleans from an English invasion. Later, the nuns told us, Joan of Arc was captured, sold to the British, and burned at the stake as a witch. But somehow, her suffering seemed worth her glory. We also learned that in the first century Childeric, the feared king of the Franks, blockaded Paris. Unable to get supplies, the Parisian people were starving to death. But St. Genevieve miraculously found enough food to feed the entire city.

The idea of being a saint appealed to me. First of all, their lives were not boring like mine. And the saints seemed to have some direct connection to God that other, "normal" people didn't have. They also possessed the ability to perform miracles, such as healing the sick (St. Blase, St. Francis of Assisi), writing great theological works despite ignorance (St. Thomas Aquinas), and persuading the not-so-Christian citizenry to melt their golden serpent into a new chalice for the church (St. Barnatus). Even though they were often tortured and killed, I loved the whole idea of the saints. They were magnificent people and their lives had profound effects on their communities. After all, it was Mother Cabrini who found water for her convent and it was Bartholomew De Las Casas who freed the Spanish slaves.[1]

---

[1] Koenig-Bricker, Woodeene. *365 Saints: Your Daily Guide to the Wisdom and Wonder of Their Lives,* HarperCollins, San Francisco, 1995.

If someone had asked me at that age, "What do you want to be when you grow up?" I would have said, "A saint."

But the larger global consciousness of the time, or at least the global consciousness I was exposed to, held that mere mortals could not aspire to sainthood. "Hardly anyone becomes a saint," I was told. "It's very hard and takes a hundred years because the church has to verify that you actually did perform a miracle."

A hundred years! I felt my aspirations fading.

"Besides," I was told, "it's not something you can decide. God either chooses you or he doesn't."

At that point, I laid my lofty goals aside and decided to be a housewife or possibly an artist. The years went by and by and by. I had completely forgotten those early dreams of sainthood until I started writing this book. Slowly the memories surfaced and took their place in the organization of my mind. In my search for the old woman of my visions, it has become increasingly clear that all of us possess the power to think great thoughts and do great deeds. All of us are capable of being that transformative agent for ourselves, our families, and our communities. All of us, just like the saints, are capable of "interceding for the people on earth."

For these reasons, my search for the old woman has not just been about finding her, it has also been about how to *become* her. Which path to walk, which thought to think, which door to open? I have tried to weave a tapestry of directions, if you will, on how we arrive at this doorstep.

Because we can.

It is interesting to me that in searching for this knowledge, the answers have often come from the past rather than the present. The knowledge of living a sacred life is embedded in stories, legends, and myths, and in the ancient religious and social traditions of many different cultures. We've had the knowledge all along. It did not need to be contrived or invented; it only needed to be found and embraced.

Which is why I sought out Angeles Arrien, Ph.D., for this book. Dr. Arrien is a cultural anthropologist. The physical, social, and cultural development and behavior of humankind is her field of expertise. As a teacher, author, and speaker, she works with cross-cultural healing traditions and devotes much of her life to ensuring that the old stories and the ancient wisdom ways are not lost or forgotten. Her own tradition, which she steadfastly follows, is that of the Basque mystics. "Basque mystical practices look to nature as mirrors of our own internal nature," she told me. "We work with singing, dancing, storytelling, and silence." In the Basque culture, the firstborn is the tradition bearer and it is his or her responsibility to pass on the cultural traditions to the new generations. No surprise that Dr. Arrien should study anthropology. She is the firstborn. "In this way," she said, "I pass on the stories and the old ways, so that they stay alive."

Dr. Arrien's book, *The Four-Fold Way,* was helpful to me in a profound way. It opened doors and gave depth to my thinking. In this book she instructs about walking the paths of the Warrior, Teacher, Healer, and Visionary, part of which I would like to share here because by walking the four-fold path, we are better equipped to take our journeys and live our lives.

Dr. Arrien said, "The Warrior's way is to know the right use of power, the Healer's way is to extend love, the Visionary's way is to express creativity and vision, and the Teacher's way is to model wisdom. Through the resource of power we are able to show up. Through the resource of love we are able to pay attention to what has heart and meaning. Through the resource of vision we are able to give voice to what we see, and through the resource of wisdom we are able to be open to all possibilities and unattached to outcome."[2]

Dr. Arrien encourages us to develop not one but all four paths in our lives. She encourages us to walk the Four-Fold Way. "Walk-

[2] Arrien, Angeles. *The Four-Fold Way,* HarperCollins, San Francisco, 1993, page 130.

ing the Four-Fold Way," she says, "means opening to the universal archetypes of the Warrior, the Healer, the Visionary, and the Teacher, which lie within us waiting to express their wisdom in all our actions and choices in the world."

After reading her book, I went to one of her classes. I was sitting in a crowded hall when she walked on stage and started reciting the passage read from Marianne Williamson's book. I will never forget that moment.

It was one of those gray and dreary days. I was feeling particularly vulnerable—swimming in doubts, fearing my future, and feeling most insignificant and small. Did I really think I could accomplish anything?

"Our deepest fear is not that we are inadequate. Our deepest fear is that we are powerful beyond measure," Dr. Arrien said in a voice most strong, most beautiful.

What? I was spellbound. Captivated. *"We ask ourselves, who am I to be brilliant, gorgeous, talented, fabulous? Actually, who are you NOT to be? You are a child of God. Your playing small does not serve the world."*

That is when I knew that Dr. Arrien held an important piece of the tapestry of this book.

But as has happened before in the writing of this manuscript, our coming together took an unexpected turn. Magic was once again afoot. *El duende* was about. I went to Dr. Arrien for the old stories, for the ancient tales, for the legends of times long ago. I wanted her to tell me what history knew of the menopausal passage.

What I came away with was something much much more. In the process of our conversations, a new story, a future legend was born. Listen now to the magic of her voice.

⚜ *Angeles Arrien* ⚜

The Lack of Story

You asked me to find stories about menopause, so I looked for the fairy tales about women when they come into menopause. I tried to find stories about the difference between the wise woman or the full woman versus the witch or the hag or the crone. I feel that menopause is a spiritual journey. It's a passage into more depth and more internal riches. So I looked for wisdom stories that instructed women in being their fullest, that told how to draw on more of the gifts and experience they carry, rather than focusing on how they are not bleeding anymore, and therefore life is over. But I couldn't find these stories. It's interesting, isn't it, that they aren't there? That there is a lack of story.

The only story I've found so far is the one I like to tell about the necklace called the "Black Nubian Woman." It is an old Sir Laurens Van Der Post story that has been collected and comes out of his collections of tales of the bush.[3] But this story can be for a woman of any age. It can be for the young maiden, or it can be a story for the wise woman. Stories are the greatest teaching art that we have. They transmit values, traditions, memories, and wisdom. And because this story is about spiritual healing, and because it applies to menopause, I will tell it here.

This story is a feminine initiation story where the Wise Woman within prompts the Maiden who comes to the riverbed to do her

---

[3] *Betwixt & Between: Patterns of Masculine and Feminine Initiation.* Edited by Louise Carus Mahdi with Steven Foster and Meredith Little; "An African Tale" by Helen M. Luke. Open Court Publishing Company, La Salle, Illinois, 1987.

healing and gather her wisdom in order to trust her own guidance and nature.

This is a story that happened a long, long time ago in a far, far, far-away land. It is a story that is older than the pine needles on the trees and it is a story that is found east of the sun and west of the moon. This story is about a beautiful, black Nubian woman who walked through her village wearing a magnificent red toga and carrying a basket on her head. She wore a fabulous necklace of ju ju beads, as it was the custom among the women in the village to wear these necklaces they had fashioned. And she had put together the most beautiful of necklaces. All the women in the village were so very jealous, not only of her beauty and her dignity and her grace, but also of this fabulous creation, this necklace, that they vowed that some day they would get that necklace away from her.

As the black Nubian woman walked through the village, she would hear the whispers and her heart became heavy as she wondered what it was that she had done that the women of the village excluded her. And yet, with great dignity and grace, she continued about her chores, even though she was very aware that there was the distancing and the separation.

Every Friday, all of the women went down to the riverbed to wash their clothing and then let it dry on the riverbanks. So the black Nubian woman, she came down, down, down to the riverbed to wash her clothing. All the other women were splashing each other and having a wonderful time, waiting for their clothing to dry on the riverbed. As she got closer and put her basket down, they turned to her and said, "Oh won't you come into the river with us? We know that we have been very unkind and unfriendly, but we would like to change that. Oh, won't you come into the river with us?"

The black Nubian woman was deeply touched and she

thought, "Oh, what a great blessing on this day." What a great blessing that she would be once again included in the sisterhood.

When she went into the river, she noticed that none of the women had their necklaces on. And she said, "Where have you placed your necklaces because I would certainly like to place mine with yours." And they said, "Oh we did a very special ritual this morning. This morning we threw our necklaces in the river as an offering to the gods and the goddesses of the river." And once again she was deeply touched and deeply moved and she said, "Oh what a wonderful thing to do, to offer your necklaces to the gods and goddesses of the river." So very slowly she reached back and took off her necklace and threw it into the river with a great prayer to the gods and goddesses of the river.

And as the necklace went down, down, down into the river and was no longer in sight, the other women turned upon her and splashed her. They laughed and giggled and jeered and said, "Oh do you think we would be so stupid as to give our necklaces to the gods and goddesses of the river? Do you think we would be so stupid?" And they went over to the side of the riverbank and pulled their necklaces out of the mud. They washed their necklaces and laughed and were very pleased with their great coup. And they put their necklaces back on and filled their baskets with their dry clothing and laughed and giggled and splashed her some more, and then went back to the village.

The black Nubian woman walked over to the side of the riverbank and she wept. She wept. Then she stood up and she put back on her red toga and filled her basket full of clothing and as she walked along the side of the riverbank, she prayed. She prayed to the gods and the goddesses of the river to return her necklace. And she prayed and she prayed.

Pretty soon she thought she heard something. At first she dismissed it. "Oh, it just must have been the gurgles in the river." But no, she heard it again.

"Plunge in. Plunge in," said the deep, deep voice. And she heard it again. "Plunge in."

Being the woman that she was, she plunged into the river. She plunged down, down, down to the very depths and landed on the bottom of the riverbed. As the mud began to clear, there about twelve feet away was this very old woman. She was sitting there with all these oozing sores. And she said in the same deep voice, "Lick my sores. Lick my sores."

The black Nubian woman touched her heart and felt for a moment, and then without hesitation, on hands and knees, she crawled along the riverbed and came in front of the old woman and picked up her hand and began to lick one of the sores. And then the most amazing thing happened. All of the sores on the old woman's body closed, and her face became very luminescent and radiant. But at that very same moment, they heard a terrible sound. Footsteps.

The old woman said, "Quick, quick, under my riverbed coat. Quick. It's the old demon of the river." And she pushed the black Nubian woman way way down underneath her riverbed coat.

And the old river demon came up to the old woman and said, "Where is she? I smell a young woman in my river. Where is she?"

The old woman of the river said, "Oh, demon of the river. You will never catch her. She went that way. About two hours ago. But you will never catch her."

And the demon ran down the river and pretty soon it was quiet. You could no longer hear the old demon's footsteps on the riverbed. So the old woman reached down and pulled up her riverbed coats and she pulled the black Nubian woman back up. And then she reached way down and she pulled and pulled again, and out of the river came the most exquisite necklace you have ever seen in your entire life. It was made of gold and silver and crystals and diamonds. The old woman washed this most beautiful necklace and then very carefully put it around the black Nubian woman's neck. And the old woman said, "Thank you. Thank you for your compassion and thank you for your willingness to heal again."

Then she clapped her hands and threw the black Nubian woman out of the river. And she clapped her hands again and out of the white foam came a beautiful white basket that landed at the side of the black Nubian woman on the riverbank. And she clapped her hands again and out of the white foam came a beautiful white toga that landed on the side of the riverbank. And then she clapped her hands again and the river went back to its normal gurgle.

The black Nubian woman wrapped herself in the beautiful white toga and placed the white basket on her head and touched her beautiful necklace of gold and silver and crystals and diamonds, and she began to walk along the side of the riverbed. As she looked into the river, she saw a reflection of herself. She saw the soul of who she was.

But soon she heard some voices. The women were coming down to the river to wash their clothing. When they saw her, they couldn't believe how beautiful she was. And they raced around her and touched her white toga and her white basket and her necklace and they said, "Oh where did you get that? It's all so beautiful."

Being the woman that she was, the black Nubian woman pointed to the river. And they ran past her. She said, "Wait," but it was too late, and they plunged into the river. They plunged down, down, down, deep into the river. And when the mud began to clear, there, standing twelve feet away from them, was this old woman and she was covered with all these oozing sores. And she said in a deep, deep voice, "Lick my sores. Lick my sores."

And they all huddled together and said, "Oh, we couldn't do that. We couldn't possibly do that." Now at that point, they heard the most terrible sound. And the old demon of the river came walking from down the river and he walked up the riverbed and he gobbled them all up. And their bones went to the top of the river.

And in that very long, long ago time, in the time when stories are older than the pine needles on the trees, in the time when stories are found east of the sun and west of the moon, they lived well and they died well.

INITIATION

Among many indigenous peoples, the woman who is going into menopause initiates the woman who is going into puberty. It comes full circle because in one the blood is being incorporated internally, and in the other the blood is just beginning to flow. There is an old wisdom in that. If your mother does not tell you about puberty, then it will be a woman who has just gone into menopause who will tell you, and who will pass the wisdom on.

I looked for a group of fairy tales where women mentor women, whether it was an older woman who taught a younger woman how to weave or spin, or whatever. Because I think therein lies the archetype or the mystery of this passage; the feminine mentoring and how that is tied around the blood mysteries.

I've found a grouping of fairy tales in which a woman passes on a handkerchief or stitches a handkerchief with a red rose in it and it's surrounded by lace. And in the story of the Sultan King, the wife initiates the man. She becomes the mentor to the man. But I wanted to find the stories where women mentor women in a positive way. Because we, like Cinderella, have not been mentored well by the women in our lives.

The stories about the good witches would be stories of the wisdom, but they are few and far between. These would be the stories in which there is an old woman you can go to for healing. Or stories of an old woman in the forest to whom you could send your children. Not the witch, not the one who will harm the children, but the one who protects the children.

I've found only one story in which this is alluded to, so that's why I think women in this culture have a hard time with menopause, and with different stages of being mentored by women. We need these stories. We need to have Grandmother stories—wisdom stories; stories of older women initiating younger women in positive and powerful ways.

CREATING THE NEW

Perhaps the tale that needs to be told is not yet written or the Grandmother stories are still in oral tradition rather than written form. In creating such a story, there would be elements of the feminine. There would be a veil, a mirror, and a comb. There would be perfume and shoes, like old slippers. And there would be a handkerchief. The handkerchief is the symbol for grief and loss. There is a sacrifice at each rite of passage. Menopause involves having to grieve the young maiden, but (wisdom is) still knowing that she's incorporated within.

There would be a glass or cauldron that would hold red wine, which would symbolize the taking in of the blood and the celebration of those mysteries.

There would be a fan that a woman could open and close. The fan is "that which has been concealed will be revealed" because a fan starts concealed and, as it opens, is it revealed. Menopause is a time that whatever has been concealed within the nature is revealed, so the fan is an important metaphor.

There would be flowers and there would be a garden.

This garden would be the garden that every woman would go to during different rites of passage in her life. One garden. The same garden. Different parts of the garden would tell you the secrets that every woman would know regardless of any passage that she would go through.

There would be the grotto of gremlins, who would be teachers about the different tests and challenges and pitfalls you would need to go through in each passage, regardless of what passage it is.

And there would be a hall of mirrors in the garden. In the hall of mirrors, a woman would get to see all the things that she had been taught about herself that weren't true. Eventually, she would come to one mirror that would totally shatter when she was willing to see who she really was in all her magnificence. The mirror would shatter and she would get to see that.

There would also be a path of hoops, arched hoops covered with garlands of flowers. There would be an archway of white roses, an archway of pink roses, an archway of red roses, and an archway of yellow roses. The white rose would take you up to when you were fourteen going into the blood mystery. The pink rose would be for when you enter into marriage or a committed relationship or have children. The red rose is for when you come into your full creativity, and the yellow rose is when the blood would be incorporated within you, when you come into the time of your life when you could manifest the golden gifts within your nature and character.

KNOWING THE DIRECTIONS

In most fairy tales, specific directions are given to find that which we long for: "Go down the road a little bit. Turn left. Go across the bridge. Just go down the road a bit and turn left. Cross the bridge. Then, you'll come into the clearing where you will find what it is that you have longed for."

It's really amazing how those instructions keep showing up over and over as a motif. Going down the road is taking a journey. Turning left is connecting to self and connecting to wisdom. The bridge is transition. (This is how you find the garden.)

The menopausal woman always has a ring of gold keys. The keys are for all the rooms that she's explored in her life and all the ones that she hasn't opened yet. And she is the one who knows how to open doors to others who come to her. This ring of golden keys is really an image about wisdom. How to open and close doors. What are the doors that need to stay closed and are not appropriate to open? In menopause, one gleans the wisdom of discernment for opening and closing appropriate doors.

All kinds of life live in the garden. Animals, birds, reptiles. They are helping allies. Any animals that have ever helped you through any rite of passage are there. The garden is also the place where the veiled woman lives. This is deeply connected to the mystery, and this is where a woman is reinitiated into veils of wisdom.

MENOPAUSE IS SELF-INITIATION

A woman will go to the garden *alone* only once in her life. That would be at this time, in menopause. All the other times she will be initiated into the mysteries of the garden. But this time, it is a self-initiation. Menopause is a deep spiritual initiation because it is the initiation that comes from within rather than from without.

The first time a woman goes to the garden is when she loses her teeth. When she's seven, because her face will change and that's the beginning of the body as a transformative cauldron. That is when both a man and a woman will recognize that this body is a transformative vehicle.

A woman will truly know that her body is a transformative vehicle when she begins to shed blood. That's the second time that she will go to the garden.

The third time will be after her first sexual experience because there is a mystery there. Many women aren't really initiated into sexuality. Neither are men. It depends on who her initiator is, whether it's a man or a woman, but that's when a woman will feel most alone. And the second time she will feel most alone is in menopause passage because they are both totally unfamiliar experiences.

The first time the blood comes out and the first time she gives birth to a child are each major rites of passage for a woman. But she always goes with an older woman in these earlier visits. And the older woman will always be different. It will never be the same older woman who takes her through each one, because the same woman never initiates the same woman in all the rites of passage.

But in menopause, she goes alone.

THE CALL

You asked what the call feels like? How a woman knows it's time to go to the garden? Sometimes it's a wake-up call. Sometimes she doesn't know, because she hasn't been listening to her dreams or inner guidance. So then it's an outer wake-up call, whether it's divorce or an accident. It could come in the form of a tragedy or a loss or restlessness, hopelessness, self-questioning. Somehow she begins to feel that sense of longing that there's something greater to be done with one's life.

To reach a place of fullness, women have to do the inner work. Two or three years before a woman goes into menopause, she should be in transition. There should be a bridging time. She should prepare to get the tools (of wisdom), to meditate, to go on retreat, or to take a day of silence.

Women who have not done any interior work before they get to menopause will be forced to go inward. The self-doubt will force them inward, and all the negative cultural conditioning will force them inward. Either they will start looking and thinking that there has to be other ways (and start on the journey), or they will regress to total denial about going through that gate and become stuck in the mode of the young maiden.

What the garden has to teach her depends on how much inner work she's already done because the garden is a cross-cultural, universal metaphor for spirituality. So there would be parts of the garden that she's never seen, and parts of the garden that she loves to see and looks forward to seeing, and parts of the garden that she hadn't remembered.

Each time the experience is different, because it reminds her of how much she has changed. She is back in the garden again, but at a different level of awareness and experience.

THE GARDEN BECOMES HOME

Earlier in her life, she comes and goes, but after the menopausal passage, a woman doesn't leave the garden. That's when the garden becomes her home. And she begins to build her own house there. Her true home. Her true nature. There is something that happens when you can no longer tolerate the false self. There is a freedom, an incredible freedom that comes as a result of leaving the false self and building a new home that really is connected to one's interior nature, which is the garden.

For a woman who is truly in the garden, her children, her husband or lover, and her friends will all find her fascinating, interesting, deep, enchanting, magical. If she's truly at home. If not, they will find her the witch. The witch is the woman who has not accepted that stage of development. She's the one who is still looking to the outer to provide satisfaction.

A lot of dissatisfaction comes from not being able to befriend silence and solitude and the richness in that experience, and expecting the exterior to still provide. The young maiden loves the external. Women who are arrested in that stage, who are stuck in young maiden, need to go inward when it begins.

As I said, sacrifice is part of any rite of passage. I think for the menopausal woman, the sacrifice is that she needs to trust. Trust.

She can't control. She may feel out of control. And that's why most women who have spent a lot of their life controlling situations have a roller-coaster ride during menopause, because they haven't cultivated the garden of trust.

RECLAIMING SELF

The body is an alchemical vessel. Menopause is a time of reclaiming who you were before puberty, before the experience of sexuality, and before the first time the hormones did their running through the body.

The finding of the girl one was before puberty might unfold like this: Before you come to the garden, there is a silver gate. There's also a very beautiful silver bell with a silver cord that the blue jay will pull to announce each time someone is at the silver gate. And so the woman comes to the silver gate and there will be a young woman there.

The blue jay is the messenger because the blue jay has no problem giving voice. And one of the initiations into the feminine mystery is to stay connected to your voice and not lose your voice. For menopausal women in particular, if as a young maiden they have not been full in their voice, they will be required to do so in the passage. No one is exempt. Every woman has to be able to bring her voice into the world. That principle is deeply connected to the intuitive nature.

So a woman is told to go see the healing woman in the garden. And she will know that she has come to the garden when she's found the silver gate and the blue jay rings the silver bell.

After she has her voice, and she's reclaimed that person she was before puberty, the garden flourishes. It becomes the most beautiful garden in the world. It's a place where people come for healing. It's a place where they come for silence. And it's a place where they gather for celebration.

It's the sanctuary where you can always go. The place where you can visit at the talking well, where you can sit and talk, and where everything you have talked about has gone into the well. That's why people throw pennies into the well, so that wishes can come true. All from the basis of those conversations that have taken place between women for centuries and how they have helped each other.

A Piece of the Tapestry

I told Angeles that my sense is that if we do this, if enough women really do the work, that we can change the world.

Absolutely. Especially if it's the women who are in menopause, who really know the gift and the opportunity that it is. Every woman has a piece of the tapestry. Every woman has a piece of the garden. But until women really understand the golden opportunity that it is, until they are willing to give up the drama surrounding their own need for attention and approval, and to use menopause that way, they desacramentalize the major spiritual initiation of their life.

But if we do it, then we become the magic women. And children know magic women. They say, "I love going to her house. It's magic." And that's where there is always food, and there are always mysterious places, and fun and creativity, and always the generative principle, always the making sure that those coming along are nurtured and assisted.

That's a big part of it. We have to do this. But instead, what's happening is that women in menopause feel like they need to be nurtured and assisted. They have it turned around. That's a woman who has not done her work. She has not visited the garden over the years. It's inward in a more narcissistic view and "look how much

I've done for everybody for years and now it's my turn" and that kind of behavior.

The healing magical woman is the woman who is full. It's not that she doesn't need that or want that, but she is committed to interdependence instead of independence.

ELDERSHIP

Women in their fifties are really in their youth of the elder years. Women in their sixties are in the midlife of eldership, and women in their seventies are truly the elders. I think that women in their seventies and eighties should be preparing women who are in their sixties, and women who are in their sixties should be preparing women who are in their fifties.

The menopausal years are really the years of being on the bridge. They are the transitional years. They are the preparatory years before going into eldership. You are in eldership when it's over. Not a couple of years before and not when you stopped your periods.

THE SHADOW SIDE

The shadow side of menopause is alive and well. Most women in this culture have been prepared for the shadow side of menopause, but they have not been prepared for the light side of menopause. We are so fixated in what's not working, rather than what is working. Menopause is considered a disease rather than a passage.

But a woman doesn't have to have difficulty in the garden. She doesn't have to escape monsters. The grotto of gremlins is there and she can spend however much time she needs to in it. The grotto of gremlins is where the false self system has to die. It will be a rough ride until she is willing to claim authenticity and look in the mirror and see she is not who she thinks she is. That's when the mirror shatters in the grotto of gremlins. And that's when she can start building her house in the garden, when she sees who she really is.

What happens usually in this phasing or staging of life is that a woman either redecorates the family home after everybody leaves, redoes it so it's just she and her husband, or creates a guest house that's hers, or a studio, or whatever. It's interesting to watch women begin to carve out a space that is theirs, where they never did before.

There's an internal flame in this garden. Like at Kennedy's grave, it never gets put out. It grows larger when a woman is willing to spend time in the garden, and it can get as large as a bonfire. Her attention makes it grow, her willingness to listen to what the fire and the flame have to say. The fire that takes no wood.

It's all about how to be able to spend time in the garden. That's why it's so interesting to me that so many menopausal women get into gardening for the first time in their lives, or get into art. It's because they need that quiet time alone. It's another way of carving out that sanctuary.

Gardening is a way of connecting to the earth. You told me earlier that you never had a garden until last year. It's amazing how this happens, but just go with it. Trust it. It's also that deep hunger for beauty and for growing things and attending to things and nurturing things that are all part of that deep generative principle.

INTUITION AND THE HEALING ARTS

As intuition increases we should be taking action. Life-affirming action. It's very important. We can listen, we can pay attention to our dreams, but if we don't take action on our dreams or what comes in meditation or through guidance or what's been revealed to us, then it will implode. That's a great source of depression.

So if a woman is experiencing depression in menopause, she

needs to be taking action on her dreams and meditations. Hans Selye says that "action absorbs anxiety." So instead of succumbing to the sleep of depression, menopausal women can stay awake through action.

Singing, dancing, storytelling, and silence are all in this garden. They are the universal healing salves. Singing and dancing are not done to try to recapture a life once had. The young maiden loves to sing and dance. But the menopausal woman sings and dances for the earth; she sings and dances for children; she sings and dances for healing. There is a ritualistic aspect to the singing and the dancing. There is a recognition that these are life force gifts that can transform or "shape-shift" environments.

I was thinking about the film, *Harold and Maude*. She sang and danced, but it was all for the purpose of uplifting Harold, of shape-shifting him, whereas if it had been a young maiden, it would have been for the purposes of seducing him. But Maude was really returning him to inspiration and to the gift of life itself.

Singing and dancing for the menopausal woman is about inspiring people to the great gift of life itself. To remind people of the joy and the essence of the celebratory spirit. And a menopausal woman will be singing her own songs.

THE PITFALLS OF ECCENTRICITY

The true menopausal woman is the one who carries dignity and grace more than eccentricity. Being like a walking cartoon rather than being oneself is not being connected to the authentic self. If I become a characterization, I am still experiencing a separation from the spiritual garden. It's almost like permission to be irresponsible is granted in that kind of cartoon eccentricity. But a true menopausal woman, one who is in the garden, is responsible and celebratory. And there is a difference.

It's interesting to think about the women who are respected by both men and women. She is the woman in the garden. She is the woman who carries dignity and grace. It's not just the woman who's respected by women, and it's just not the woman who's respected by men but not women, it's the woman who's respected by both men and women. And by children.

She will never really be alone because of how she's handled her own passage. People recognize that she's full and they want to be around her. They find her enchanting.

THE SKELETON

The skeleton is in the garden, but it's the dancing skeleton, where death is a friend. It's a friend because it prepares you for the place of no gardens, the place of golden light. It's a great teacher, where you have no fear of death, but you want to learn.

The skeleton stands for the essence of what is. The true essential nature of what is. It's where you hear the Grandmother's healing song: "Na, na, na, na, na, na, na."

The Grandmother's healing song is part of the lullabies of the world. It's tied into the blood woman's mysteries. Men will hum and sing, but the singing voices of the cradle and the singing voices of the coffin are usually the women's voices.

In the garden, we have to say good-bye to certain things. We have to let go. Every rite of passage involves sacrifice. So menopausal women should use the burying rituals or boxing rituals. Put things like clothes you can no longer wear into a box and bury them. It's a way of letting go of the outer young maiden who is being incorporated within.

Again, it's the skeleton on the bridge. By doing these actions, these rituals, you are saying: I am going to make this sacred. I am returning it back to the earth. And when we return something to the earth, we incorporate it into ourselves. I have an old garment that I have outgrown. It's an old identity, an old aspect of myself that I have outgrown, but rather than just throw it away, I incorporate it into my body, into my presence, so that it is added to me rather than taken away.

MEN IN THE GARDEN

The men are allowed to come through the golden gate. And the gold gate has a bell that is a gong. So whenever you hear the gong, there is a man making himself known at the gold gate. But he always has to sound the gong before he comes in or before he is invited in. There is that respect.

Men have their own gardens, as such, but they like caves. So a man would have a cave. And it would have many rooms within. We would have to knock or be invited in, as well. When men hit this phase of life, they have to take a similar journey.

And the man who can't handle that phase will often reach for a younger woman. He can't go into the cave by himself. If he has difficulty accepting the aging process and death, an older woman is a reminder to him that it's coming. So the younger woman shows up. It happens because the young maiden hasn't been initiated by a woman. She doesn't know because usually she's been initiated by men.

So women need to initiate women. We can change this story. It would take a full generation, but it's a very good thought. All we have to do is start paying attention. Start being with the younger women and modeling integrity instead of victimhood.

ACCOMPLISHING YOUR DREAMS

Menopause is a time for honesty. It's very interesting for women who have been in their creative fire all along or in their dreams a lot—their task is to befriend the silence or to befriend what it is like not to be doing that dream all the time. There is a balancing factor that comes in menopause. Where maybe there has been excess in one, that begins to decrease. And where there's been dormancy, there's an increase. Women who have been out there in the trenches tend to go deep inside. They don't want to be out there anymore. Women who have been more inside or tending to family want to go outside. There is always this balancing.

There is a time that Margaret Mead called postmenopausal zest. It is all that creative fire that gets ignited. Many women in their fifties come into their dream because they now have time to apply their energy to their dream. Family needs have been attended to and now they have the time to be the bonfire. Dreams that have been put on the back burner all of a sudden come to the front burner. They are not going to wait anymore.

So I would like to encourage women not to give up their dreams. Menopause is a time to act out or live out their dreams.

The story that follows is a new legend, a new fairy tale, inspired by my conversations with Dr. Arrien and the other women in this book. It is for all women who are in the "Red Moon Passage" and for their husbands and children and friends. And it is a story that came to me by way of the wind.

Rosetta's Garden

BONNIE J. HORRIGAN

ONCE UPON A TIME in a faraway land very near to here, there lived a young maiden whose name was Rosetta. And she lived well.

Her days were filled with the things of life: loving her husband, raising her children, tending the family home. Things like gardening and weaving, caring for her ailing mother, and visiting the graves of those who had gone before. And she was happy. And life was good.

Whenever she had a problem, which she sometimes did, she would go visit the Old Woman who lived deep in the forest. Together, they would walk in a secret place and the Old Woman would tell her stories. The Old Woman would sing, "Hei ya, hei ya. No, na, na. Ya, na, na." And after a while, her troubles would be over.

And so the days passed and the years passed and the decades passed. One morning, Rosetta woke up with an unfamiliar yearning. She felt restless and strange. "What is this?" she said. But no answer came.

Later that day as she was making soup, she thought she saw something out of the corner of her eye. "What is this?" she said. But when she turned, no one was there.

The very next morning, quite unexpectedly, her husband took ill. He was burning with fever and shivering with chills. She felt scared and alone. But she said, "Oh, I will go see the Old Woman in the woods. She will know what to do."

So she ran deep into the woods to the Old Woman's home. "Help me Old Woman," she said. "My husband is very ill."

The Old Woman took her hand and led her into the secret place. Together they walked in the gardens and the Old Woman sang, "Hei ya, hei ya. No, na na. Ya, na, na." Then the Old Woman reached deep into her pockets and drawing forth a bundle, said, "Go home to your husband and make him tea from this root and bread from this wheat. Then take him to the cave by the river. Let him sleep there alone for three nights."

And so Rosetta went back to her husband and made him tea from the root and bread from the wheat. Then she took him to the cave by the river. "Sleep here for three nights," she said.

"Won't you stay with me?" her husband asked.

"No," she answered, even though it pained her to leave.

She went home, and she worried and fretted and paced, but she did not go to the cave. Finally, after three long days, her husband returned in good health.

And life went on. And life was good.

Then one day as she was making soup, she thought she saw something out of the corner of her eye. "What is this?" she said. But when she turned, no one was there.

A few days later her son fell ill. He was burning with fever and shivering with chills. "Oh," she said, "I must go see the Old Woman in the woods." Off she ran, deep, deep, deep into the woods, until she reached the Old Woman's house. She knocked on the door, as she always had before. "Old Woman, help me," she called. But no one came.

She opened the door and stepped in. "Old Woman, help me." But no one was there.

Rosetta sank to the floor and began to weep. The Old Woman was gone. Without directions, she would never find the secret place. Without the songs, she could not heal. Without the root, her son would die. But as she wept, she thought she heard something in between her tears.

"Go down the road," the voice whispered. "Go down the road."

Rosetta looked out the door, into the woods. Go down the road? Alone? But she had never gone that deep into the forest before. Who knew what dangers lay ahead? What ambushes? What storms? "No, I cannot go," she answered.

But the voice, which sounded to her like the Old Woman's voice, whispered, "Go down the road."

Gathering strength, Rosetta stood up and went out the door and went down the road. And she went even farther down the road. After she crossed the bridge, she came to a beautiful silver gate. And there, growing beside it, was the most beautiful, most fragrant golden rose. She had never seen this gate before, but she felt certain it led to the secret place.

As she approached the gate, a blue jay alighted on a nearby tree. "Whoever enters here must sing," the bird announced.

Rosetta thought about the Old Woman's song and she reached deep into her mind and opened her mouth and sang, "Hei ya, hei ya. No, na, na. Ya, na, na." But instead of being beautiful and full, the song came out like a squeak. "Oh, dear," she said. So she planted her feet firmly on the ground and took a very deep breath and opened her mouth to try again, and this time she thought of healing, this time she thought of her son and his pain and his need and of his soul, and she sang, "Hei ya, hei ya. No, na, na. Ya, na, na." And the silver gate opened.

There were three paths ahead of her. One led to the east, where the sun was rising. One led to the south, where the sun shone directly overhead, and one led to the west, where the sun was beginning to set. As she stood there, wondering which direction to go, she thought she saw something out of the corner of her eye. But when she turned to the west, nothing was there.

Looking down the path into the twilight, looking into the space where nothing was there and something was there, Rosetta decided to go west.

But as she walked along the path, looking for the root and the wheat, she began to feel frightened. What had she done? The sun was setting and the night was getting closer. Shadows were beginning to form. What had she done? All of a sudden, she stumbled and fell.

Picking herself up, dusting herself off, she saw that what she tripped over was a bone. A bone. With a strange hunger, she began to dig. Soon she found many bones, and the bones were the skeleton of a small girl. Remembering what it was like so many years ago to be so young and so beautiful and so full of new life, she felt sad that she would never be so young again. And a tear fell from her eye.

But being who she was, knowing that she could never have what once was, only what was yet to come, Rosetta buried the bones. And as she gave the bones back to the earth, another tear fell from her eye. And another. And another. But still, she gave the bones back to the earth.

Suddenly, in the place where her tears had fallen, a garden began to grow. And there grew the root and there grew the wheat she needed for her son.

Gathering the root and the wheat, Rosetta turned to go home. "I will make him tea and I will make him bread and I will sing to him so that he will sleep the healing sleep," she said.

But then she had another thought. "Who am I that I think I can do this?" she wondered. "Who am I that I think I can heal? Really, who am I?"

With that thought, she looked around in despair. But the Old Woman was not there.

Then out of the woods came four deer. Each was carrying a mirror, which they laid at her feet.

She picked up the first mirror and looked at her reflection. She thought she was going to see a beautiful young maiden in the fullness of life, or a mother cradling a young son, or a woman weaving a beautiful veil. But what she saw was a dead rose. Not believing her eyes, she picked up the second mirror and what she saw was a dead rose. And she picked up the third mirror and what she saw was a dead rose. And she began to weep.

The fourth mirror lay on the ground.

Being who she was, as her tears fell, she thought about her son who was burning with fever and shivering with chills. So she closed her eyes and she opened her heart and sang, "Hei ya, hei ya. No, na, na. Ya, na, na." But she was not singing for her son. Not yet. This time she was singing for herself, that she might be brave, that she might sleep the braving sleep.

And when the song was over she opened her eyes and looked in the fourth mirror. This time, she saw through the mirror, through her own eyes. And then she saw through her son's eyes and she saw through her husband's eyes and she saw through her mother's eyes. She saw through the eyes of her village, and she saw through the eyes of her country, and she saw through the eyes of the world. And the mirror shattered in her hand, for she no longer needed it to see.

She hurried home then, through the woods and through the night, home to her son. And she made him tea from the root and bread from the wheat and she sang him the healing song so he would sleep the healing sleep.

And then Rosetta went and laid beside her husband, who smelled of the cave, and she closed her eyes. And in her dreams, she went into her garden and planted a golden rose. And in her life, a rose grew.

And life went on. And life was good.

PART NINE

Ariadne's Thread

Long ago in ancient times, the people of Athens suffered a terrible fate. To stop Minotaur, a fierce monster that was half-man, half-bull, from destroying their land, they were forced to pay tribute to the king of Crete. To keep Minotaur at bay, King Minos demanded that each year he be given seven Athenian lads and seven Athenian maidens.

With great sorrow, a lottery was held in Athens each year, and the chosen youth were sent to Crete on a ship with black sails. Once there, King Minos fed them to the monster Minotaur. It was a time of darkness and the people of Athens grieved for their sons and daughters.

On Crete, the monster Minotaur lived in a complex labyrinth so skillfully contrived that no one, not even the cleverest of humans, could find his way out. Minotaur roamed this labyrinth, feeding on the Athenian victims placed there by King Minos.

And as long as he was fed, all was well.

When Theseus, the king of Athens' son, returned home from his adventures and discovered the terrible fate that had befallen his country, he vowed to slay the monster and stop the slaughter of his people. So he offered himself up as one of the seven lads. His father grieved, but Theseus was determined.

The following year, the ship departed under black sails. But Theseus waved from the deck and promised that he would return as the victor under sails of white.

When the youths arrived in Crete, they were paraded before the king. Theseus was a handsome, charismatic lad and as fate would have it, the *king's daughter, Ariadne, became deeply enamored of him. Wishing Theseus to live, Ariadne secretly furnished him with a sword to slay the monster and a clew of thread to mark his trail so when the deed was done, he could find his way out of the labyrinth. And so it was that Theseus slew the monster Minotaur and delivered the people of Athens from their terrible burden.*[1]

There is very little left to say.

I chose the story of Theseus and Ariadne to begin this final chapter because it is a story about liberation from fear. It's a story about finding one's way.

Rather than be shackled by fear, Theseus chose to face that which threatened his world. When he sailed off to Crete, it was without guarantees. He did not know how he would slay the monster. But as often happens when a person acts according to his heart and follows the voice of his soul, help arrives from unplanned sources.

For Theseus, this magical aid came from a woman, from the feminine. Ariadne gave him a sword—the means to kill the monster—and a clew of thread, the means to escape from the ever-tangled abyss.

I believe this story tells a lesson about *authentic* journeys that we can never learn too well. So often we feed our children, our beloved dreams and creations, to the monster in an effort to keep the boring, cruel, sorrowful, empty, desperate status quo of our lives intact. And who can blame us? It's frightening to think about what would happen if we declare that we won't pay the ransom anymore. We are taught by our culture that some terrible fate awaits if we fail to comply.

But modern times are full of misconceptions. What should be clear, what we should be teaching ourselves and our children, is

---

[1] Based on the story of Theseus, as written in *Bulfinch's Complete Mythology,* Spring Books, London, 1989, pages 109–112.

that if we let go of our fears and bravely follow our hearts, *help* awaits us.

Now, I am not saying that this "help" will make everything easy, or that you no longer have to participate in your own life. Quite the opposite. Remember, after Ariadne gave him the sword and thread, Theseus *still* had to enter the labyrinth and fight Minotaur, and he *still* had to use the thread to mark and recover his way out of the tangled abyss. He had to take his journey. But with Ariadne's help, he was better prepared.

I am also not saying that following one's heart means forgoing one's responsibilities. It is actually quite the opposite. Theseus's journey was about his responsibility for his own life and the lives of *all* the Athenian people. It was about his responsibility for his culture and country.

In this context, letting go of one's fears and following one's heart may not be easy, but it will lead one to a new and more rewarding way of being, one where a ransom doesn't have to be paid. I remember having lunch with two psychologists back in 1990. They were from the Colorado Woman's Healing Project, and both were attuned to spirit. I was writing a story on the new women's psychology that was emerging and where it was leading us, and we were consequently discussing journeys of the soul. These two women told me that it was hard to get their patients to follow their hearts because the first thing that always happened was that everything fell apart. So it looked like, it *appeared* that, listening to one's intuition and following one's heart was only going to get one in a heap of trouble. This is the point where a lot of women stop, they said. This is when women abandon their journey and head back to the safety of things that are known.

But should women keep going? I asked. Isn't it dangerous? The two psychologists smiled and told me that when they were able to help a woman stick with her decisions and stay on her heart path, things usually worked out quite well.

I've never forgotten that conversation or that wonderful insight. Keep listening to your heart, no matter what. Don't lose faith. Because the help that arrives can usher in new realities. It can free you from your own Minotaur and deliver your children, your creations, to the world.

My own story is a good example. Years ago I was struggling with a deep despair over being childless. I felt this welling sorrow, no matter how vain, at the aspect of my youthful appearance transforming into a wrinkled, bent form, and remorse about losing my potent energy without having accomplished my dreams or giving birth to my children. I lived with the terror of growing old and dying a death that was the end of all ends, the type of end that harbors within it no new beginning.

I was trapped by these fears, powerless to change. The monster of old age could not be slain.

Then I was visited by an aged woman who showed me another possibility for reality in which the ending was a beginning. Dancing magically in the air, she beckoned me to bring her forth, to give her voice. And so it was that my help arrived.

Not being a sage, only a student, I sought out eight women whom I admired and asked them to speak the truth. What is menopause? Who is this old woman? Which path leads out of the labyrinth of fear?

These women implored me to look beyond surface appearances to that which forms the form. They instructed me to study the wisdom of ancient myth and religion, to connect with the unconscious underworld and listen to my soul, and above all, to release my fears and embrace the journey, to keep walking the path.

And so I sailed to my own Crete.

Many things both strange and wonderful happened to me in the process of facing my fears and bringing the old woman to light. That I should conceive and give birth to my only son at the age of forty-three while researching this book about a passage that marks the close of a woman's fertility may seem to be a rather silly paradox. But I believe it illuminates and gives form to the most profound understandings these women offered.

Life is changeable. Life is alive.

The Red Moon Passage is a long journey that is normally made between the ages of forty and sixty. At some point during that time a woman will stop menstruating, but if one is open to all that life offers, that is not the total experience. If one is available, if one is connected to the deeper aspects of being, a major transformation of consciousness happens in synchroneity with the biological change.

In this way, menopause is a sacred state. It is a point in our lives when the veil between the ordinary river of our existence and the "river beneath the river"[2] grows thin. It is a time when we are psychically and spiritually open. Should we choose, we have access to a special transformative power during these years.

More than likely you will not become pregnant with a child, as happened to me, but rather this potent energy will fill your being with some other gift. For those who are willing to walk the path, the challenge is this: We must find out what it is we are called to do with this special power and then we must do it.

The myths and legends clearly tell that as elder women, we possess the wisdom and power to see, hear, and feel the truth. The teaching stories say that we are able to give birth on a universal level to those things we conceive in our hearts. This is a bold statement. It means that it is possible for us to actually change reality for ourselves and others . . .

- by "singing over the bones"[3]
- by "integrated to-one's-toes" thinking

[2] A phrase coined by and excerpted with permission from Clarissa Pinkola Estés, *Women Who Run with the Wolves.*
[3] Ibid.

- by "thanking in advance"
- by "licking the old woman's sores"
- by "reimaging" the future
- by bringing our ideas "from heaven down into the earth"
- by using the magical transformative energy that is available to those who live in "a state of grace"

By using these tools, we can create a new future. We can change that which needs to be changed. And this is both a wondrous gift and an awesome responsibility.

So I ask: If you were Grandmother Spider, if you could speak a world into being, what would you say? If you could sing a dream to life, which dream would it be?

The women I spoke with, and who have now spoken to you, offered great insight and provided a much needed light for our journey's start. They have given us a sword by which we can slay the monster and the light of wisdom needed to find Ariadne's thread.

Dr. Estés once told me that Ariadne's thread is a metaphor about intuition. The thread enabled Theseus to "see around corners." In life, this ability to make the right choices in the face of many unknowns flows from our connection to our souls, and it is this connection that will lead us out of the darkest traps.

Let me interject here that it is not my intention to oversimplify a complex issue. This book does not explore the many trials and tangents involved in becoming conscious co-creators of our lives, nor did I intend it to do so. That is your task should you decide to make the passage.

What this book does try to do is point the way for menopausal women to transform from beast to beauty. What I hoped to achieve by this writing was to name the possibility.

Before I end, I would like to share one final vision I had while making shamanic journeys to the other side of reality. It may help in the passage and it may shed further light on the concept of co-creation and our understanding of the magical realms, and thus be of service during these years.

The vision came in June 1990, when I was exploring the idea of creation and co-creation and what it meant to be able to manifest one's dreams and ideas. Before I took the journey, I asked to be shown the truth, no matter what that truth was. This is what I experienced.

I am caught in a dangerous, fast-flowing river. Feeling scared, I swim to the edge of the river and climb out. I breathe heavily, grateful to be alive.

As I sit on a ledge above the roaring river, a bird flies down and lands beside me. He tells me to jump back in.

"I can't," I say. "I will die in that river."

"You will also die here on the ledge," the bird remarks.

I look around me at the towering cliffs and know the bird is right. If I stay on the ledge, I will eventually starve. The only way out of the canyon is to ride the river. Yet who could survive such a thing?

"Jump back in," he says again.

The bird is my spirit guide, so even though I feel doomed, I trust him. I jump back in the roaring waters.

In the turbulent currents, I am thrown against the rocks. My skin is cut, my bones are bruised. I try to fight back and can't, the river is too strong, so I finally let go of all my resistance to the experience and allow myself to be tossed about. If I am to die, I will die.

As I let go, the river calms. Now I am floating in a peaceful river, being carried along by gentle currents. As I ride these warm waters I try to feel what the river feels. I try to see the canyon through its eyes and feel the world through its heart. Soon my consciousness melds with the consciousness of the river. I am the river.

Something ineffable happens. I decide to have the river turn to the left instead of the right. The cliffs part and the river goes left. I decide to have the river go up instead of down. And the river goes up.

And then I am back in my body, lying on my living room floor next to the fireplace.

This particular journey had a profound effect on me. When I returned from the other world and regained ordinary consciousness, I was deeply aware that I would never view life in the same way. But one of the most remarkable understandings was that the decisions and choices I made about the river when I was an individuated soul sitting by its side and the decisions and choices I made about the river *as the river* were entirely different.

So this is my final gift to you. This is what is what I was taught about trust and this is what I was taught about my true connection to all of life.

In closing, I just want to repeat that *everything you do matters.* Life is alive. Life is changeable. And so I ask one more time: If you were Grandmother Spider, if you could speak a world into being, what would you say? If you could sing a dream to life, which dream would it be? And if you were the river, which direction would you flow?

Good luck on your journey through menopause. I hope you are able to find your way out of the labyrinth into the land of wonder that awaits us on the other side of the Great Divide.

·❨ ABOUT THE CONTRIBUTORS ❩·

≋ *Jeanne Achterberg, Ph.D.* ≋

Jeanne Achterberg is a psychologist, research scientist, and healer. She is a professor at Saybrook Institute and senior editor of *Alternative Therapies in Health and Medicine,* and was on the faculty of Southwestern Medical School for eleven years.

BOOKS
- *Bridges of the Bodymind* (IPAT, 1980)
- *Imagery and Disease* (IPAT, 1984)
- *Imagery in Healing: Shamanism and Modern Medicine* (Shambala, 1985)
- *Woman as Healer* (Shambala, 1991)
- *Rituals of Healing: Using Imagery for Health and Wellness* (Bantam, 1994)

AUDIO
- *Imagery in Healing* (New Era Media)

≋ *Paula Gunn Allen, Ph.D.* ≋

Paula Gunn Allen is a professor of English at the University of California, Los Angeles. She is also a poet, storyteller, and shaman.

BOOKS

- *The Sacred Hoop: Recovering the Feminine in American Indian Tradition* (Beacon Press, 1986)
- *Spider Woman's Granddaughters: Traditional Tales and Contemporary Writing by Native American Women,* edited by Paula Gunn Allen (Fawcett Columbine, 1989)
- *Skin and Bones* (West End Press, 1989)
- *Grandmothers of the Light* (Beacon Press, 1991)
- *The Woman Who Owned the Shadows* (Aunt Lute Books, 1991)
- *The Voice of the Turtle: American Indian Literature 1900–1974* (Ballantine Books, 1993)
- *The Song of the Turtle: American Indian Literature 1974–1995* (Ballantine Books, 1995)
- *Life Is a Fatal Disease,* with Patricia Clark Smith (West End Press, 1995)
- *As Long as the River Flows: Nine Native American Heroes* (Scholastic Press, 1995)

Angeles Arrien, Ph.D.

Angeles Arrien is an anthropologist, teacher, and founder of the Angeles Arrien Foundation for Cross-Cultural Education and Research. To contact her office, call (415) 331-5050.

BOOKS

- *The Tarot Handbook: Practical Applications of Ancient Visual Symbols* (Arcus Publishing, 1987)
- *Wheels of Tarot: A New Revolution,* edited by Angeles Arrien and James Wanless (Merrill-West Publishing, 1992)
- *Signs of Life: The Five Universal Shapes and How to Use Them* (Arcus Publishing, 1992, winner of the 1993 Benjamin Franklin Award)

- *The Four-Fold Way: Walking the Paths of the Warrior, Teacher, Healer and Visionary* (HarperCollins, 1993)

AUDIO
- *Universal Aspects of Healing*
- *Sacred Portals: Dreams, Meditation and Creativity*
- *The Art and Craft of Storytelling*
- *The Spiritual in Ancient and Modern Storytelling*
- *Power and Love in Relationship*
- *Change, Conflict and Resolution from a Cross-Cultural Perspective*
- *Gathering Medicine: Stories, Songs and Methods for Soul Retrieval*

⁂ *Clarissa Pinkola Estés, Ph.D.* ⁑

Clarissa Pinkola Estés is a senior Jungian psychoanalyst, award-winning poet, *cantadora* (keeper of the old stories) in the Latina tradition, and radio commentator for community public radio. She is the former director of the C. G. Jung Center for Education and Research in the United States and the founder and current director of La Sociedad de Nuestra Señora Guadalupe, a human rights organization.

BOOKS
- *Women Who Run with the Wolves: Myths and Stories of the Wild Woman Archetype* (Ballantine, 1992)
- *The Gift of Story: A Wise Tale About What Is Enough* (Ballantine, 1993)
- *The Faithful Gardener: A Wise Tale About That Which Can Never Die* (HarperCollins, 1995)
- *Myths and Stories of the Wise Old Woman Archetype* (forthcoming from Alfred A. Knopf, late 1996)
- *The Collected Poetry of Clarissa Pinkola Estés* (forthcoming from Alfred A. Knopf, early 1997)

AUDIO

Clarissa Pinkola Estés, Ph.D., is the creator of a collection of original audio works combining myths and stories from her family with archetypal analysis, psychological commentary, and her acclaimed poetry. Titles include:

- *The Faithful Gardener: A Wise Tale About That Which Can Never Die* (90 minutes)
- *Women Who Run with the Wolves: Myths and Stories on the Instinctual Nature of Women* (180 minutes)
- *The Creative Fire: Myths and Stories on the Cycles of Creativity* (180 minutes)
- *Theatre of the Imagination,* a 12-part series of myths, stories, poetry and psychological commentary broadcast over many NPR and Pacifica radio networks nationwide (1,080 minutes)
- *Warming the Stone Child: Myths and Stories about Abandonment and the Unmothered Child* (90 minutes)
- *The Radiant Coat: Myths and Stories on the Crossing between Life and Death* (90 minutes)
- *In the House of the Riddle Mother: Archetypal Motifs in Women's Dreams* (180 minutes)
- *The Red Shoes: On Torment and the Recovery of Soul Life* (80 minutes)
- *The Gift of Story: A Wise Tale About What Is Enough* (60 minutes)
- *The Boy Who Married an Eagle: Myths and Stories on Male Individuation* (90 minutes)
- *How to Love a Woman: On Intimacy and the Erotic Life of Women* (180 minutes)

For information about these and forthcoming audio releases by Dr. Estés, write or call Sounds True Audio, 735 Walnut St., Dept. RMX, Boulder, CO 80302. Telephone (800) 333-9185.

﹏ *Bonnie J. Horrigan* ﹏

Bonnie Horrigan is a journalist and the publisher of the medical journal *Alternative Therapies in Health and Medicine*. She has studied shamanic healing for ten years. She may be reached at P.O. Box 3043, Olivenhain, California, 92024.

﹏ *Kachinas Kutenai* ﹏

Kachinas Kutenai is a registered nurse, Apache medicine woman, teacher of all ages, and human relations counselor. She is the founder of the Sacred Rainbow Circle, which is dedicated to teaching Native American ways, offering alternatives to racism, sexism, and speciesism while honoring Mother Earth's needs. To contact Kutenai, or for information about books, videos, and other current and new releases, please write to the Sacred Rainbow Circle Foundation, P.O. Box 26892, San Diego, CA 92196–0892.

BOOKS

- *Medicine Woman Speaks: A Simple Instruction to the Use of Herbs* (Sacred Rainbow Press, 1981)
- *American Indian Healing: Only the Strong Survive* (Sacred Rainbow Press, 1990)
- *Buffalo Spirit Rising: A Modern Medicine Woman Looks at the State of the Earth* (Sacred Rainbow Press, 1996)

VIDEO

- *Healing the Emotions, and Herbs, Vitamins and Minerals* (Sacred Rainbow Productions, 1992)
- *Spending a Day in the Sacred Way* (Sacred Rainbow Productions, 1992)
- *Storytelling: All My Relatives* (Sacred Rainbow Productions, 1993)

AUDIO
- *Thirteen Steps to Forgiveness, Atonement and Healing* (Sacred Rainbow Productions, 1995)

☀ *Carol S. Pearson, Ph.D.* ☀

Carol Pearson is the dean and a distinguished human and organizational research scholar at Mount Vernon Institute in Washington, D.C. Telephone (202) 625-4506, fax (202) 338-4261.

BOOKS
- *Who Am I This Time? Female Portraits in American and British Literature,* with Katherine Pope (McGraw-Hill Book Co., 1976)
- *The Female Hero in American and British Literature,* with Katherine Pope (McGraw-Hill Book Co., 1981)
- *The Hero Within: Six Archetypes We Live By* (Harper & Row, 1986)
- *Educating the Majority: Women Challenge Tradition in Higher Education,* with Donna Shavlik and Judith G. Touchton (ACE/Macmillan Publishing Co., 1989)
- *Awakening the Hero Within: Twelve Archetypes to Help Us Find Ourselves and Transform Our World* (HarperCollins, 1991)
- *Magic at Work: A Guide to Releasing Your Highest Creative Potential,* with Sharon Seivert (Doubleday, 1995)

☀ *Jamie Sams* ☀

Jamie Sams is a Cherokee and Seneca writer, songwriter, and poet. She is the founder of the Native American Tribal Traditions Trust and Earth Medicine Foundation, which benefit Native Americans and the children of the earth.

BOOKS

- *Medicine Cards,* with David Carson (Bear & Company, 1988)
- *Sacred Path Cards* (HarperCollins, 1990)
- *The Sacred Path Workbook* (HarperCollins, 1991)
- *Other Council Fires Were Here Before Ours,* with Twylah Nitsch (HarperCollins, 1991)
- *The Thirteen Original Clan Mothers* (HarperCollins, 1993)
- *Earth Medicine: Ancestors' Ways of Harmony for Many Moons* (HarperCollins, 1994)

AUDIO

- *Voices of the Wild: Lessons and Medicines of the Animals* (Sage Brush Productions, 1995)

Barbara G. Walker

Barbara Walker is a writer and feminist.

BOOKS

- *The Woman's Encyclopedia of Myths and Secrets* (Harper & Row, 1983)
- *The Secrets of Tarot: Origins, History and Symbolism* (Harper & Row, 1984)
- *The Barbara Walker Tarot Deck* (US Games Systems, Inc.)
- *The Crone: Woman of Age, Wisdom and Power* (Harper & Row, 1985)
- *The I Ching of the Goddess* (Harper & Row, 1986)
- *The Skeptical Feminist* (Harper & Row, 1987)

- *The Book of Sacred Stones: Fact and Fallacy in the Crystal World* (Harper & Row, 1989)
- *Women's Rituals: A Sourcebook* (Harper & Row, 1990)
- *The Women's Dictionary of Symbols and Sacred Objects* (HarperCollins, 1991)
- *Amazon: A Novel* (HarperCollins, 1993)
- *Feminist Fairytales* (HarperCollins, 1996)
- plus ten books on the subjects of knitwear design and knitting patterns

·◖ BIBLIOGRAPHY ◗·

Achterberg, Jeanne; Barbara Dossey; Leslie Kolkmeier. *Rituals of Healing: Using Imagery for Health and Wellness,* Bantam, New York, 1994.

Allen, Paula Gunn. *Grandmothers of the Light,* Beacon Press, Boston, 1991.

————. *The Sacred Hoop: Recovering the Feminine in American Indian Tradition,* Beacon Press, Boston, 1986.

Arrien, Angeles. *The Four-Fold Way: Walking the Paths of the Warrior, Teacher, Healer and Visionary,* HarperCollins, San Francisco, 1993.

Black Elk, Wallace. *Black Elk: The Sacred Ways of the Lakota,* Harper-Collins, San Francisco, 1990.

Branston, Brian. *Gods of the North,* Thames & Hudson, London, 1955.

Brown, C. Mackenzie. *The Book of the Goddess, Past and Present,* Crossroads, New York, 1992.

Bulfinch, Thomas. *Bulfinch's Complete Mythology,* Spring Books, London, 1989.

Campbell, Joseph. *The Hero with a Thousand Faces,* Anchor Books, New York, 1977.

————. *The Power of Myth,* Anchor Books Doubleday, New York, 1988.

Douglas, Alfred. *The Tarot,* Penguin Books, New York, 1972.

Drury, Nevill. *Dictionary of Mysticism and the Occult,* Harper & Row, San Francisco, 1985.

Duerk, Judith. *Circle of Stones: Woman's Journey to Herself.* Lurame-dia, San Diego, 1989.

Encyclopedia of Eastern Philosophy and Religion. Edited by Stephan Schumacher and Gert Woerner. Shambala Press, Boston, 1989.

Estés, Clarissa Pinkola. *Women Who Run with the Wolves: Myths and Stories of the Wild Woman Archetype,* Ballantine Books, New York, 1992.

Gimbutas, Marija. *The Language of the Goddess,* HarperCollins, San Francisco, 1989.

Harner, Michael. *The Way of the Shaman,* HarperCollins, San Francisco, 1990.

The I Ching or Book of Changes, third edition. Translated by Richard Wilhelm. Princeton University Press, 1950.

Itule, Bruce D. "Growing Up Apache," *Arizona Highways,* September 1992.

The Jerusalem Bible, Doubleday, New York, 1968.

Jung, C. G. *The Basic Writings of C. G. Jung,* The Modern Library, New York, 1959.

Koenig-Bricker, Woodeene. *365 Saints: Your Daily Guide to the Wisdom and Wonder of Their Lives,* HarperCollins, San Francisco, 1995.

Locke, Raymond Friday. *Sweet Salt: Navajo Folktales and Mythology,* Roundtable Publishing, Santa Monica, 1990.

Luke, Helen M. "An African Tale" from *Betwixt & Between: Patterns of Masculine and Feminine Initiation.* Edited by Louise Carus Mahdi with Steven Foster and Meredith Little, Open Court Publishing Company, La Salle, Illinois, 1987.

Matthews, John, ed. *The World Atlas of Divination,* Bulfinch Press, Little, Brown and Company, Boston, 1992.

Mullett, C. M. *Spider Woman Stories: Legends of the Hopi Indians,* University of Arizona Press, Tucson, 1991.

Murphy, Cullen. *Woman and the Bible,* Atlantic Monthly Press, Boston, 1993.

Pearson, Carol. *Awakening the Hero Within: Twelve Archetypes to Help Us Find Ourselves and Transform Our World,* HarperCollins, San Francisco, 1991.

———. *The Hero Within: Six Archetypes We Live By,* Harper & Row, New York, 1986.

Ressner, Phillip. *Jerome the Frog, Parents* Magazine, New York, 1967.

Sams, Jamie. *Earth Medicine: Ancestors' Ways of Harmony for Many Moons,* HarperCollins, San Francisco, 1994.

Sams, Jamie, and David Carson. *Medicine Cards,* Bear & Company, Santa Fe, 1988.

Standard Dictionary of Folklore, Mythology and Legend, first edition. Edited by Maria Leach. Harper & Row, San Francisco, 1972.

Walker, Barbara G. *The Crone: Woman of Age, Wisdom and Power,* Harper & Row, San Francisco, 1985.

———. *The Skeptical Feminist: Discovering the Virgin, Mother and Crone,* Harper & Row, San Francisco, 1987.

———. *Women's Rituals: A Sourcebook,* Harper & Row, San Francisco, 1990.

Woolf, Virginia. *To the Lighthouse,* Harcourt Brace & Company, London, 1927.

·❨ INDEX ❩·